MANAGER IN SHORTS

THE SHOCKING TRUTH ABOUT PEOPLE MANAGEMENT AND LEADERSHIP

Practical guide, useful tips and theoretical background to professional people managers, specifically in the high-tech industry.

There is no framework for management nor for leadership but there are principles and there are tools.

More importantly there are priorities and focus. In this book I'll share my thoughts on what's important and what's not. What differentiate between being a good people manager and a great one.

Gal Zellermayer

I'd love to hear from you. Feedback, questions, tweets - I read everything and always reply, even if it might take a few days. You can reach me via email at gal.zellermayer@gmail.com or at Twitter @galzellermayer.

Table of Contents

Chapter 0
Metadata - don't skip this time

YOU DON'T SUFFER FROM IMPOSTOR SYNDROME; YOU SUFFER FROM THE DUNNING-KRUGER EFFECT

6 MINUTES READ

I *know, I know. I too usually skip this part or just browse it really quickly in order to mark it as read, while not spending any quality time on it. Why should you care about the metadata behind the book? Why would you care about the reason I wrote this book, or even more stupid - how to read it? You know how to read. It's not the first time you are doing it...It's idiotic.*

You are not wrong. But you are not completely right.

I kept this part really short and I assure you that spending the time now will make the read of the book more enlightening, fun, effective, and useful. That's it. I've made my pitch - your turn to decide if you bite or not.

PURPOSE

The purpose of this book is to make you think.

This book is not a recipe or a script that will take you hand-in-hand to the promised land; I don't believe such a book exists.

This book will make you think.

It will force you to challenge your current behaviors, it will throttle your beliefs: is Gal right? Is he full of bullshit? Does it even make sense?

This thinking will help you shape your management style and design your leadership agenda.

This book will take you out of your comfort zone, which is the only way to do disruptive growing.

I will share principals, guidelines, tools, methods, and ideas on how to become a better manager and an exceptional leader.

You might find in this book several things you didn't have a clue about, some other things will look familiar.

I guarantee though, there would be at least a handful of **ideas that will rock your world**.

This book will help you shape your management style and to understand the right priorities for being a leader. It will provide clarity.

I'M A MANAGER IN SHORTS

As a leader, you and only you, need to design the self-portrait of your management style.

What are your beliefs? What are your specific values? How do you interact with the people that report to you? How do you communicate with your colleagues? On what are you willing to compromise? What are your clear red lines? What would you fight for? With whom are you eating lunch? How do you speak? What do you emphasize? Are you using ethos? What is your dress code at work?

Me? I'm a manager in shorts.

Both in the way I dress, but also in the way I talk, interact, and give feedback - everything is very short, concise, direct, and sometimes even blunt.

No distance on the one hand, but not the class clown either.

I like to swim against the current. People often call me a thought provoker. I love it. I like to have **strong** opinions. Strong opinions, but **loosely held**.

I'm a manager at heart. I believe that people management is a profession, not a step on your career ladder and, of course, not a necessary evil.

My passion is for building great software teams that can deliver wonderful products.

I get inspired when the people I've coached are advancing, growing, and learning.

That's just me.

You need to find your own management style. Build it, work on it, and adjust it as you go.

7 SENTENCES ON MYSELF AND ON MY LIFE

I'm married to Limor, who is the love of my life and my inspiration. We met at the university where I studied bioinformatics, and she was on the Dean's List of the computer science department.

Later on, Limor had a similar career path to mine - from a software developer to a team leader, and a group manager.

I'm always asked how is it to have your significant other work in the same industry as me, in the same role (and lately in the exact same company, OMG!)?

The short answer: It's amazing!

We usually come home after work and have dinner with our 5- and 8-year-old crazy boys. After tucking them in to sleep, we get comfy on the living room sofa.

Then, instead of watching *Game of Thrones* or *The Good Wife,* we discuss and brainstorm about our work - I can get advice on a conflict I've had with a colleague or a challenge I'm facing in building the strategy of the group.

Then we pour a glass of rose wine, or grab a cold beer while watching *Game of Thrones*.

MY CAREER IN A NUTSHELL

I've been around the tech scene since 2003.

I've done QA, written code, managed small teams and large groups.

I've worked in small startups (Trivnet), mid-sized companies (Dropbox), and corporates (EMC, VMware, Facebook).

I took part in waterfall development and ran agile organizations.

I've mentored and coached, people in my team, colleagues, and other leaders in the industry. For a more detailed bio see my LinkedIn profile.

YOU

This book is beneficial for anyone who is working in a management or a leadership position. Or consider doing so in the future. Actually, if you care about people this book is for you.

You probably don't suffer from Impostor Syndrome.

You might be suffering from the Dunning-Kruger Effect

Most of the excellent tech leaders and managers I know think they suffer from Impostor Syndrome. They are wrong.

*Impostor Syndrome (also known as **Impostor** Phenomenon or Fraud **Syndrome** or **Impostor** Experience) is a concept describing high-achieving individuals who are marked by an inability to internalize their accomplishments and a persistent fear of being exposed as a "fraud".*

In almost every leadership conference that took place in the last couple of years and on a monthly basis in twitter or blog posts, you can catch a person from the industry showing and speaking about how they are suffering from Impostor Syndrome.

What's going on here?

Why do so many managers and leaders feel they are less knowledgeable and less capable than their peers?

Well, the answer might be a bit different than what you think...

Do you know how most people managers become people managers?

It is not because they are great at managing people. It is because they were great at their previous role as individual contributors - engineers, QA, designers, whatever - and they felt they could not "advance" in their role anymore. But they were good. And the organization didn't want to lose them; so, the organization "promotes" them into people management positions in order to retain them.

We will double-click on that sequence later.

For now, the important thing to understand is that people managers, after switching modes from a maker to a manager, feel that they don't have the ability to make low-level decisions. They are right....

This is not Impostor Syndrome. This is just reality. It happens to all kinds of managers - good, bad, seasoned, and green. As people managers drift away from the hands-on doing (whether it is coding, designing, or testing) it is a natural thing to feel. In the chapter on decision making, we will learn how to cope with that state and with the accompanying feeling.

There is another phenomenon, much more disturbing. It has almost the opposite effect as Impostor Syndrome. It is called the Dunning-Kruger Effect and some managers in our industry suffer from it.

*"In the field of psychology, the **Dunning–Kruger Effect** is a cognitive bias wherein people of low ability suffer from illusory superiority, mistakenly assessing their cognitive ability as greater than it is. The cognitive bias of illusory superiority derives from the metacognitive inability of low-ability persons to recognize their own ineptitude; without the self-awareness of metacognition, low-ability people cannot objectively evaluate their actual competence or incompetence." (Wikipedia: The Dunning-Kruger Effect)*

Putting this in simpler words - when you don't know a lot, you don't even know that you don't know. When you know quite a lot, you know enough to know that there is a lot you don't know. *Maybe it wasn't simple after all.*

One of the reasons I wrote this book is to help great managers to focus on what's important. Scope out the irrelevant things. Provide tools and tips to move from good into exceptional and also to make sure you feel that what you are doing is real, important, and not a fake. If you suffer from Impostor Syndrome this should help you to cope.

Another reason I wrote this book is to help managers increase their self-awareness by putting bluntly in front of them only the things that are important, forcing them to rethink their beliefs, and reevaluate their own performance. As Sheryl Sandberg (the chief operating officer of Facebook and founder of Leanin.org) said: "We cannot change what we are not aware of, and once we are aware we cannot help but change".

In Tasha Eurich research (PhD, is an organizational psychologist, researcher, and *New York Times* best-selling author) described also in HBR article from October 2019 (*HBR: Working with People Who Aren't Self-Aware*) they have *"discovered that although 95% of people think they're self-aware, only 10 to 15% actually are."* If you suffer from the Dunning-Kruger Effect (you don't know you do) it would help you.

This book will make you aware.

HOW TO READ THIS BOOK?

This book is divided into chapters. Each chapter can stand by itself and will give you an isolated agnostic value.

In each section, you will see an estimated reading time. If you are a very fast reader, or tend to skim-read, the time would be much shorter. However, **this book, as you'll see soon, is supposed to intrigue deep thinking. Thus, the recommendation here is to take your time. Let the ideas sink in, digest.**

Create an inner argument in your head. Re-read it and shape your beliefs.

Each chapter starts with a real-life example or a story designed to get you in the right mood. Then, it continues with the theory. The theory is critical for deep understanding. Most of the chapters end with practical tips and tricks.

A WORD ABOUT DIVERSITY AND INCLUSIVENESS

I care deeply about diversity. Why? Due to several reasons, but the most important one was articulated by my admired manager in the past, Uri Nativ (today, he is the VP of engineering of the startup Torii). When Uri was asked why he invests time in making the hi-tech industry a more diverse place, he answered: "Since I can".

There is tons of research and articles showing how diverse teams are more innovative, creative and well... with diverse thinking. But that is only part of the picture. The other part is the will.

The will to make a difference. The will to make the world a tiny bit better. So, if you have the analytics justification and the will to make the world better, the only thing left is the power to make a difference. As hiring managers, as people managers, as thought-leaders, we all have that power to make a difference. Let's use it.

In this book, I have tried to use a diverse language, so sometimes I'm referring to her, sometimes referring to him, and sometimes to them.

Likewise, I've tried to take examples that have involved a diverse range of employees.

This book was reviewed and edited - both from the language perspective and from the content perspective - by Limor, my wife who as I mentioned above also has extensive engineering management experience. I hope that her view helped me and this book to be a bit more inclusive.

If you spot anything that you think is offensive or not inclusive, please let me know in gal.zellermayer@gmail.com and I'll adjust accordingly.

Chapter 1
The (legacy) manager's principles

IT ALL STARTS HERE

A few years back, I was a team leader, working for a mid-size American company.

I completed 2 consecutive positions at this company, managing a team of 5-7 software developers and quality engineers building different products in the domain of monitoring application infrastructures and hybrid cloud environments.

At some point I've felt that my challenges and ability to impact were exhausted and I wanted to move on from a team leader position to an engineering group manager, leading other people managers.

It was a BIG jump, but I felt ready. At some point, after I gathered enough courage, I climbed up the curved steps to the 2nd floor where the office of the site lead was located.

The glass door was wide open, and I stepped in casually asking the site lead if they have 5 minutes for a non-urgent meeting?

They were in the middle of downloading some new version of Docker to try it out for themselves, closed their 12-inch Dell laptop, moved their eyes away from the big screen, relaxed back on their big office chair, interlaced their hands supporting their neck, and stretched their legs on top of the grey wood desk.

The site lead, even though they are not the coach-like persona, are full of charisma, and a really sharp and fast thinker.

They took a whip from their electronic cigarette and then said that it seems to them that I'm a good fit for the role, but currently there are no relevant openings.

Dejectedly and naively I've asked "well....OK... but I'm kind of bored. What should I do now?"

Instinctively they said that each manager should aim to master 4 domains: T & 3 Ps:

- **Technology** - you know: coding, design, architecture, databases, frontend, and so on.

- **Product** - what are we building and why?

- **Process** - plan and execute.

- **People** - (-:

"In this order" They added casually.

The site lead said that until an opening emerged, I should master these.

Such an opportunity did arise a few months later and I was promoted. But we are not here to talk on my career path but to learn about the principles of management.

Years later, I've used the same manager's principles, in different order, when mentoring and shaping engineers into management roles. Actually, it has been useful not just for developers who wanted to be managers, but also for individual contributors that wanted to find their weak areas and to identify their sweet spots.

Also, it helped me find my own weak and sweet spots and to build my own personal development plan. Personal Growth Plan (PGP).

While doing the research for this book, I found similar frameworks by industry leaders. One that resonated with me was framed by **Lido Anthony "Lee" Iacocca**. He is an American automobile executive best known for spearheading the development of the Ford Mustang in the 1960s. This is what he had to say about managing a business:

"In the end, all business operations can be reduced to three words: people, product, and profit."

I think he was almost right.

Chapter 2
PUPPET - The new manager's principles

PEOPLE CULTURE PROCESS PRODUCT
BUSINESS TECHNOLOGY

5 MINUTES READ

T he principles the site lead told me about - T & 3 Ps - have a good flow. It is simple and really easy to remember.

But, life is not as anal as our boolean software paradigms... and as much as I like KISS (Keep it Simple, Stupid) approaches, these 4 principles didn't support all the use cases.

When narrowing it down, two issues bothered me the most about the T & 3 Ps principles.

The principles were lacking agility and accuracy. If not elaborated the legacy principles are a bit rigid. Rigid in the sense that the same principles, the same templates, should always apply no matter for which organization the manager is working or the manager's experience or their exact role.

As an example - I've always felt that as a very junior team leader with just two or three developers reporting to, the importance of the product understanding is almost an epsilon (and here I don't necessarily mean understanding what the feature is, but deep understanding of the market fit, the product vision and strategy, the business and so on); but the importance of my technical capabilities are critical in this role as a team leader.

On the other hand, when I'm managing 4 scrum teams, 25 people, 3 architects, and 5 quality engineers, then, it's really not that important that I'll be the best technologist in the room. Understanding the business needs becomes much more important.

The same reasoning applies when speaking about the *process* section of the manager's principles. While managing a small team of engineers, the ability to create the right processes for that team is crucial for their day-to-day practice. Once you are managing 3 teams of 20 engineers, process skills are important but are not sufficient. You need to have the ability to create the right culture for your team to operate in.

Why? Well, we will dive deeper into that in chapter 4, but just as an appetizer, a process that would be great for a team that is developing UI components - thus requires, for example, an extensive attention into UX details - is not relevant for a team that handles infrastructure work. But in most cases, these two completely different teams can have the same culture guidelines for keeping high quality if that's important for the business.

Julia Grace, an engineering director in Slack, had similar thoughts that were articulated much better: "Behaviors that made you a great junior (manager) are not what will make you a successful senior (manager)"

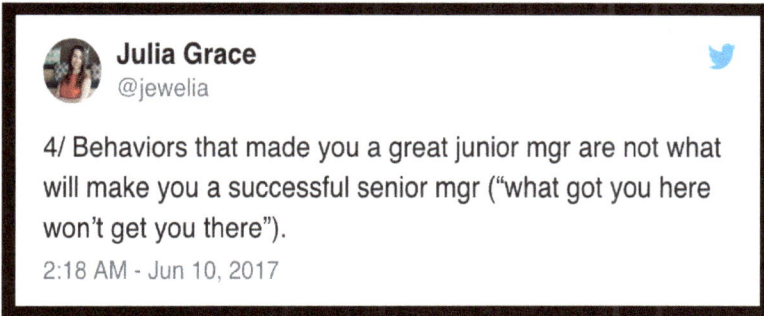

Julia Grace
@jewelia

4/ Behaviors that made you a great junior mgr are not what will make you a successful senior mgr ("what got you here won't get you there").
2:18 AM - Jun 10, 2017

Roughly speaking, I think we can divide the management world into 3 different roles of management.

The first one is a junior engineering manager - this is a team leader that typically manages 2-8 software developers. Some companies refer to them as first line managers or front-line managers. They should have at least some level of hands-on day to-day-activities.

The second role is in the range of a senior engineering manager, a group leader, a director in a medium-size company, or a VP of engineering in a startup - they usually manage indirectly 9-30 people and also manage people that manage people.

Lastly, we can think of a VP of engineering of a mid-size company, a general manager in a big company or a site lead for a large organization, and so on.

Thus, I've come to realize that the manager's principles should be more agile, almost something that would feel stretchable according to your exact role, company type, seniority, personal tendency, and organization's needs.

For that and for other reasons, I've enhanced the manager's principles just a bit and gave it a catchy name (I hope) - PUPPET. PUPPET - People, cUlture, Product, Process, businEss, and Technology.

Yes. I know there is already a configuration software/company that is named that. If you find a better acronym feel free to DM me and I might include that in the next version of the book and give you appropriate credit.

The next four chapters in this book are going to cover the entire PUPPET principles for managers:

People - Why you should drop everything else and focus on people's development - chapter 3.

cUlture and Process - When in doubt, think culture! The secret of turning a good team/group/company into a great one - chapter 4.

Product and businEss - Why should managers care about the company's mission and goals? - chapter 5.

Technology - The shocking truth about "hands-on" managers and the lies you've been told about it - chapter 6.

In each one of these chapters, I also explain how the agility of the principles comes to play.

Chapter 7 to 9 of this book would be dedicated to give a taste of extra skills and practices that are beyond the PUPPET principles, and go deeper into the important art of decision making and 1:1 meetings.

Chapter 3

It's all about the People

WHY YOU SHOULD DROP EVERYTHING ELSE AND FOCUS ON PEOPLE'S DEVELOPMENT

THE FIRST AND MOST IMPORTANT P IN THE PUPPET PRINCIPLES FOR MANAGERS - 35 MINUTES READ

A decade ago, while I was working as a developer and a Scrum Master, I had a coffee break with the team Product Owner (PO; this is a flavor of a Product Manager that handles mainly inbound issues).

The PO started her career as a brilliant developer, and after a few years in software, and later on doing user experience work, she shifted to product management.

As we usually did on those breaks, while she was working hard on her deconstruct cappuccino, we had chatted about various things - the last TV show that was running, the extremely hot and humid weather we had then in the middle of July, and the next planned vacation. But mostly, we had been gossiping about work. We were complaining. Trash talking.

The funny thing was, that we had worked in a great company, on a very interesting and challenging product and technology. The benefits were great. What did we have to complain about?

Something wasn't right.

We'd started meta talking about our complaints. We are both kind of positive people (at least, compared to the average high-tech clinician pessimist).

After she has worked 2 more minutes on preparing for herself another deconstructed cappuccino, we came to the conclusion that we both felt that we were not growing. At least, not at the pace that we wanted. We didn't get almost any feedback about our day-to-day work. The recognition we got was nominal, if at all. The people that were managing us had more of a technical leader persona and were not equipped in people management skills.

It felt that my team leader should have been a Product Manager. The Product Manager was more fit to be an Engineering Manager. The Chief Architect was better suited to be the Site Lead, and the Site Lead should have been the CPO.

Some of the developers clearly needed to move into management positions, and some of the group leads had zero leadership skills but were great technologists and their hands-on skills were just missed.

This staffing chaos not only caused less than optimized results, but also triggered the sense that career paths in the company are not managed in the right way.

A recent pulse survey came up with extremely negative results. Showing that people were not motivated, engagement level was low, and the overall satisfaction was not even close to the industry standards. We'll talk more about the pulse surveys later, but for now know that these are employee satisfaction anonymous polls that give the organization a heartbeat on the overall satisfaction of the team.

This had only reassured our coffee chats' conclusion. People development, growth, and well-being are not the organization's focus.

Luckily, the company understood that there was a problem, and was also ready to give us enough freedom in order to try and mitigate it.

In the following weeks, the Product Owner and I volunteered to be part of a 5-person cross-functional work stream that had the mandate to improve the basics of the situation. In the first meeting of the work stream we tried to identify the goals - what should be our first focus. The PO and I had simultaneously shouted - IT'S ALL ABOUT THE PEOPLE.

It took me a while to really get it. Once I got it, it took me some more time to say it out loud. But, once I did - it was the most liberating feeling in the world. **Managing is all about the People.**

Let me say it again: **It's all about the** People. It's about caring for them, guiding them, mentoring and coaching them and building them to success.

People as individuals, and as a team.

If you'll have to take just one key take-away from this book, please take this one:

The most important thing you need to do as a Software Manager is to improve the skills of your engineers and to improve the performance of your team. Make them better!

Don't do anything else, before you have invested enough energy in making the team a better one.

This is probably true for all leaders and managers of highly skilled individuals working in high-tech-like industries (knowledge workers).

If this is crystal clear to you - rock on! This chapter might help you with some practices, tips and tricks on how to do that. But basically, you have already found a safe land in the raging ocean.

The reality, however, tells a different story. When you ask most software managers 'what is their most important task?' or if this is too abstract, 'how are they spending their day?' there is a wide variety of different answers. Here is just a random list of answers I've picked from my colleagues: help the team meet the deadline, make the technical decisions, set the project milestones, solve conflicts inside the team, be responsible for cross-team collaborations, help the product managers groom the product backlog, provide status report to the leadership, seeing the big picture and more...

All these are important, they are all part of the things you might need to do, but you have limited time and capped amount of energy, so when you need to prioritize where to invest your big money first, the answer is clear - invest your time and energy in people's growth.

You need to have the right people, working on the right things, in the right way. In this order.

SO WHY DO PEOPLE MATTER SO MUCH?

People matter so much, since it is a win-win equation.

Let me discuss 3 trivial facts that lead to a non-trivial conclusion.

Trivial fact number 1 - if you invest in people, in developing their skills and improving them, they will be better engineers.

They will write better code, they will have better communication skills, they will understand the big picture, they will understand customer's view and they will earn leadership skills.

A few years back, there was a great viral meme running through Linkedin A CFO is asking the CTO:

 - *"Why should we invest so much time in training our engineers?"*

 - *"Think what happens if we don't invest in them - they will leave our company and then go to other companies." The CTO answered with a peaceful mind.*

 - *"But what will happen if we invest in training them and they leave anyway?" the CFO didn't let go.*

The VP of R&D (vice president of Research and Development which is usually responsible for the engineers in the company) who'd casually listened to the conversation jumps in:

 - *"Think about what will happen if we do **not** train them and they stay..."*

It is unclear where this meme has started but the earliest I could find can be contributed to MartinRisgaard in a tweet from 2012 - https://twitter.com/Risgaard/status/238914803022843905?s=20

Trivial fact number 2 - A happy worker is a better worker.

Trivial fact number 3 - A Challenged worker is a happy worker.

Non-trivial conclusion - A challenged worker is a better worker!

Isn't keeping the people happy good enough? Isn't that what's important?

It is very important to keep employees happy - it's mandatory even. If they are not happy, they will leave.

It turns out though, that keeping employees happy is not enough. Yes, it is mandatory but is it just not enough.

The reason is that there are a lot of excellent places of work which people would think of as interesting and welcoming. However, there are not a lot of places with great managers.

But no one likes to be out of his or her comfort zone. Challenging people, giving them feedback, constructive as it would be, might make them uncomfortable. It would take them out of their comfort zone and might make them unhappy?!

Indeed, it is a tricky thing to manage.

Great managers are willing to invest their time and energy in mentoring and coaching the people on their teams. Also, they have the skills and capabilities to teach and to cultivate the right culture that would allow this kind of growth. They understand that with mentoring and coaching focus, they can identify developers that are not doing well enough - Is it solving problems? Is it writing elegant code? Is it understanding the customer point of view? Great managers will spot these things and will invest time and energy with the developers to create a plan on improving these.

An organization that is able to establish such a great management layer would benefit from the fact that the engineers would be better developers with a deeper and wider skills set. This almost goes without saying. However, the by-product of that is surprising and overwhelming - **it turns out that people, at least highly skilled people, would like to learn and to improve.**

According to [Daniel Pink](), author of ["Drive: The Surprising Truth About What Motivates Us"]() - **mastery, autonomy, and purpose are the 3 qualities for incentivizing knowledge workers in a creative environment**.

In the last 10 years, I've probably interviewed several hundreds of candidates for engineering positions. I've done this either as a technical screening or on soft skills capabilities. One of the questions I always ask near the end of the interview, right before I leave enough time for the candidate to ask whatever is on their mind is:

"Why us?" (if it's in Dropbox then, why Dropbox, or if in VMware why VMware and so on).

The answers can vary, but I've found out that there are several common answers for talented candidates. I can't remember even a single time, that a talented software engineer answered this question without mentioning growing and learning as one of their top attributes for choosing the ideal workplace.

People want to "master their craft". Why?

HOW IS MASTERING YOUR CRAFT PUT YOU IN THE ZONE?

Only once I'd started the research for this book, I came to realize why so many leading tech companies, at least those with clear mission statements, and definitive culture, choose "master your craft" as one of their values.

The mastery is important, not just for the purpose of doing a better job - creating a performant code, or a better design - well, that is important as well... **But the real secret is that mastery helps you feel in the flow.**

"In _positive psychology_, **flow**, also known as **the zone**, is the _mental state_ of operation in which a person performing an activity is fully immersed in a feeling of energized focus, full involvement, and enjoyment in the process of the activity. In essence, flow is characterized by complete absorption in what one does, and a resulting loss in one's sense of space and time." _(Wikipedia: Flow (psychology))_

When the work that you are doing is flowing, when you are in your (comfort) zone, you feel happy. The reason for this immediate feeling of happiness is that it's easy. You feel accomplished.

Think about learning a new language, how hard and frustrating that feels? Now, think about speaking in your mother tongue - you don't even need to think about that. It just flows.

You probably remember the wonderful scene from *The Social Network* movie - Jesse Eisenberg, the main actor, who plays the network CEO, doesn't let anyone distract a developer that has been **wired in**. This developer is flowing. He is in the zone.

"Being in the flow" or *"in the zone"* - This is the same phrasing basketball players are using to describe a mental state they are in during an amazing performance.

In the book Michael Jordan: The Life by Roland Lazenby, Jordan is quoted from a TV interview where he was asked about being in the zone: "It's like every move, every step, every decision you make, it's the right decision".

So, flow is one thing, but the interesting thing here is that the mastery part works the other way as well.

One of the tech leads in my group asked me casually while we were on our lunch break, eating Humus in the site's cafeteria:

- "Gal, why do you do it? Why do you invest the time in giving this hard feedback? It must consume a lot of energy."

This was just a few days after I spent a full hour giving him very detailed feedback on the way he is stressing out the team.

- "I have no choice. This is my job." I answered trying to remove the pathos from this statement, and the Coriander from my teeth.

There is no way around that. If you are professional managers and you take pride of your work, and you master your craft, you understand that you need to set high expectations and give constant feedback in order to support people in getting there.

Simple. **It is your job.**

In the case of management, the mastery part is being a great people manager, a respected leader, and a dedicated coach. When you are accomplishing that, then and only then, you are a master at your job. It means, that as a manager and a leader, you need to focus on developing your own coaching skills and your mentorship abilities.

On the same exact point, you can see a great <u>article</u> posted in Harvard Business Review in July 2014 by <u>Monique Valcour,</u> who has a Ph.D. in Management and extensive experience as a coacher. Valcour calls the post "You Can't Be a Great Manager If You're Not a Good Coach" and describes in detail the skills a manager needs in order to succeed like the ability to listen, to ask instead of telling, build acceptability, and more.

By the way, going back to the first thought in this book - a deep understanding of what your true job as a manager really means is essential for getting some of the Impostor Syndrome out of the way. You should not feel bad about it, or to feel this is a side project, a necessary evil, or just nice to have.

I'll sign this with a "right on the money" quote I've borrowed from Tom Peters in his book *The Excellence Dividend*: *"Your principal moral obligation as a leader is to develop the skillset of every one of the people in your charge"*.

COACHING AND MENTORING - WHAT'S THE DIFFERENCE AND HOW DOES THE DYNAMIC OF THE PUPPET PRINCIPLES COME TO PLAY?

The literature suggests subtle differences between coaching, mentoring, and managing performance.

Coaching is the act of working with an individual on a specific matter that needs to be resolved.

Mentoring is wider, and a bit less defined. It's a continuous action of chaperoning one that is new to the role, or with less experience on part of it. It is almost defined by the connection between the mentor and the mentee and not by the act itself. In Japanese martial arts, you can sometimes see that as being phrased by the **Senpai** (先輩, "Earlier colleague") and **Kōhai** (後輩, "Later colleague") bond.

Managing performance might be the most common form of the three. It is kind of an evaluation of specific performance by a manager, followed by suggestions or action items to keep or to improve on.

If that is not enough subtleties, there are also plain old teachings and guiding.

Obviously, all of the above have commonalities and in practice, the differences are not as clear as the theory.

I believe that as you are broadening your scope and growing in seniority of your management role, you should move away from teaching, and guiding into coaching and mentoring. As you are managing and leading more senior peoples, specifically when you are managing other managers or leaders, they require less (not zero, but less) teaching and guiding on micro issues. They do, however, require a lot of mentoring, and coaching. They already know for example how to build a great process, so they would not need you to find pitfalls, in their work. However, you can never learn enough on the "right" culture and how to maintain it (see more about it in the next chapter).

The skill and action of giving feedback, however, which in my sense is kind of the glue between guiding and mentoring, should always be part of your toolbox.

WHAT ARE THE GROWTH AND PERFORMANCE DEVELOPMENT AREAS YOU SHOULD WORK ON WITH YOUR PEOPLE?

The short answer: everything that you see as work-related, and that you have some unfair advantage on.

The longer and more complicated answer: it depends on your role and scope; you first need to understand what is important to you and to your organization and focus on that.

Your first time as a junior (line) manager, your unfair advantage would be around your superb technical skills and domain knowledge. Later on, this would become a disadvantage as you grow away from the code. Don't worry! You'll find other topics to focus on - surprisingly, these will be more important, harder to self-learn, and also harder to teach and coach on. Some examples can be the importance of communication and how to do it right, how to increase one's impact and more.

But it's not just your exact role and position that defines the exact mentoring and coaching you should focus on. It is also the people you have in the team.

If **the team has a new engineer** fresh from college, you should invest the coaching time in teaching him how to write good quality code, exposing him to new technologies, having him understand the basics of your organization development methodology, and in becoming a communication expert (communication is everything, so you don't want him to have bad habits from the starts).

It's important to mention that, if possible, you don't have to be the one that actually does that coaching, but you should be the one that points out the importance of that and assist on the facilitation. Maybe assign the right engineer to be his mentor.

If **you have a senior engineer** in your team you should make sure she has enough impact on the organization: she should be doing knowledge sharing (not only in her team); she should be a well-known mentor (not only in her group); you can guide her to own at least one expertise, something that she is better than the rest of us. Help her find her strengths and utilize them, her superpowers.

With senior engineers specifically it is important to get them involved in their growth and career development; they usually already have a good understanding of themselves and have enough context on software and the organization, so they should lead the process of growth and only use the manager as a leverage for that growing process, but not as the one that actually does it for them.

Going back to your self-portrait - if you are a senior manager (or director), and you have team leaders in your group, you should teach them how to coach. Teach them how to develop their team members. How to coach their team.

Mentor them to be communication enablers, and not the one that is responsible for their team's communication. One of the hardest challenges for being a good manager is to move from owning the actions themselves into teaching others how to do them, while keeping the accountability for everything.

When it comes to communication, for example, the easiest thing to do for a manager is to send weekly emails with the status of the project. But, the right thing to do, is being more of a communication enabler, delegating this action of sending a status mail to the project leads or developers. As a manager, your role is to explain to the project members why that mail is important, who are the stakeholders that should get it, and what a good mail template looks like. This is just one example out of many.

One nice framework you can think of is the [Dreyfus model](#) for skills. It's a good way to understand the different levels of skills your teammates are positioned to help them grow accordingly. The Dreyfus model basically split your skill levels into 5 categories (novice, advanced beginner, competence, proficient, and expert) and your mental state in 4 functions (recollection, recognition, decision, and awareness); the model then does a binary match between the level of seniors to each function quality.

It doesn't really matter which framework you are choosing. The idea is to think about the ideal software engineer – then try developing and coaching your team members to be such.

Note that an ideal software engineer in one place might not be ideal in a different company, so you need to make sure your expectations are aligned with the organization you serve. On the other hand, as you'll see down the road of this book, you should have some expectations that are basic and common for all the great developers out there.

I, as an example, think of the ideal developer as a Joker - kind of the jack of all trades - the one that can write great code but is also able to create and present an appealing presentation to a customer if needed.

The person that can resolve a conflict with the right organization diplomacy touch and can share her technical knowledge so her team can be jokers as well. Hence, I need to invest in all the Joker traits when giving feedback.

AM I AN HR PARTNER?

I had the privilege of presenting my ideas on the basic and most important job of the engineering manager - the people part.

I've presented that in large conferences, in small evening meetups, during interviews for leadership positions, and in the amazing restaurant we have on the site, talking with a colleague.

In this entire time there wasn't even a single person who claimed I was wrong. Instead they were asking a much more controversial question:

"Isn't that the job of an HR partner?" or "why do I need you if I have a great human resource person in my organization" or in a different notion "are you saying that I can bring to this job a manager from the marketing world or the finance one?"

My own brother even asked me once, weather I really think that being a management's master with zero technical experience can replace me at my work?

You should not avoid this question or feel offended by it. It is a good question. It should make you think.

And the answer, as of most good answers is actually quite simple.

It doesn't matter who is the person that is doing the job of people development, as long as it is done greatly.

In my eyes, to do it great, the best thing is when it is done by an engineering manager, someone with an engineering experience, that speaks the same language as other engineers, and knows how to spot their comfort zone, their blind spot, and to guide them how to use them or discover them.

Can an HR partner do that? Probably yes, to some extent, but they would lack the deeper understanding on what's really important when you are a software developer and how to improve what's needed to be fixed.

Can a manager from the finance world do it? They can do some part of it, but would a manager from the finance world understand the real passion of a software developer? Would they know how to guide an engineer to develop their general debugging skill and not focus on learning just another programming language?

So, the answer is that it doesn't matter who does the job of developing people, of building teams, it's just a matter of who is the best skilled person for the job.

When the conversation gets heated - and from my experience, these kinds usually do - I ask a controversial question myself: "Would you put on that job a great engineer with extreme technical capabilities, but with no people skills and zero self or social awareness"?

Obviously, the answer is no, unless the one asking the question is that developer with the zero self-awareness.

THE PRACTICE - HOW TO MENTOR PEOPLE, HOW TO GIVE FEEDBACK?

Mentorship, coaching, and feedback are huge topics that can and have been discussed over several books, but I like to give several important tips.

TIP: Push the engineers out of their comfort zones but not all the time

People's growth, in general, happens much quicker if they are out of their comfort zones.

You must be more creative to survive in an unfamiliar territory; also, it is safe to assume that the areas they should improve in the most, are areas where they feel less comfortable in.

I know it's a cliché, but I'll state it here anyhow, since it is very difficult to apply - Engineers (and humans in general) will not like the fact they are being pushed away from the stuff they are doing best.

Also, the organization might not like it, since for the short-term the ROI (Return of Investment) will be negative.

Still, this is the place where you need to stand on your ground - both with the employee and with the organization. It is part of your professionalism.

I know that on the surface, the idea of pushing people out of their comfort zones might look confusing and maybe even contradictory. We've said above that people would like to be happy, and being away from the comfort zone is by definition not a fun place to hang out in.

But you need to remember that **flow and growth are two different things**.

It is very hard, maybe even impossible to achieve both of them at the same time.

As a manager you would be doing a good job if you can have your developers doing some of the work in a flow state, and some of the work in a growing state - this will ensure reasonable ROI for the organization in the short-term, happiness and mastery from the engineers, but also the growth and the development parts of the equation. I'm elaborating more on the differences between flow and grow in the example below.

TIP: Be explicit and blunt about it

I'm sure that everything I've just explained about growth, comfort zones, and feedback is not new to you.

You already know most of it.

The only thing I've done here was to put it clearly and define it as **your** job, as your role. It is part of your mastery. I'm explicit and blunt about it (see what I did here?!).

The thing is, ICs (Individual Contributors) which are not managing people, most often do not grasp right away that as their manager your job is to set expectations and give them feedback. This is one of the reasons you need to say it explicitly and out loud: **I'm here to give you feedback, I'm here to help you grow.**

- Declare it as your role.

- State your intention clearly.

Now, act on it!

For each person, you should invest time to understand what is the path for her and how should she get there - what is the best way for you to coach her?

Also, be explicit when your feedback goes directly to performance improvement or measurement, and when it is more connected to career development and personal growth.

Sometimes performance and growth are related, overlapping, or even the same, but sometimes they are not. Imagine for example the following scenario:

You have a backend developer with 5 years of experience.

As part of his career path, he would like to become a full stack engineer. In order to achieve that, he needs to learn front-end development. Fortunately, in his last project, there were aspects both of backend and of front-end development.

When you are going to give him feedback on the project it would probably make sense to separate your basic expectations from him as an experienced backend developer versus the room for him to grow as a front-end/full-stack engineer.

So, you can think about letting him know that the way he designed the backend components was very clear and simple, but you've expected him to be more detailed on the API signatures. This is the feedback on the current expectations from him.

Meanwhile, it was impressive to see how fast he learned the React framework and concepts, and in the future, it would be good if he can extend the set of tools he masters in, for having his work delivered a bit more rapidly. This is coaching on the growth part of the equation.

TIP: As a manager, you are an enabler for their self-development; you are not in charge of it

As a people manager, you are not the one that can do the real work when it comes to people's growth.

You are an enabler for the development of the people, but you need to throw the real effort on them; you can think about your role as their lighthouse – you should light the right way, but they should do the sailing, and eventually they decide, which boat to buy, how to paint it, what is the velocity or speed, and where to go.

If they are not into that, if they don't care about their performance improvement, if they don't care about continuously improving, about growing their skills, you need to try to sell the importance of it to them. You can do that by creating a direct line from growing into advancing their career or increasing their satisfaction and so on.

If they still put up resistance, in my experience, for the long-term you are going to have a problem. Engineers, as skilled as they are, without the need and will to grow, would not be motivated and it would be hard for you to keep them engaged for a long period. If you can't change that mindset after a few months you should try to think of alternatives for that developer (different team, company, role, etc.).

For the developer that has the right passion and motivation to grow, you need to light the way. Coach them on differentiating between the important stuff that lasts and the buzzwords that would fade next week. Teach them how to think about a career path, mentor them on increasing their circle of impact.

TIP: Performance management - focus on impact and output and not on effort

A few months ago, while I was driving from the office back home to pick up my 2 young boys from kindergarten, I got a call from a colleague of mine -

an Engineering Director for a large cybersecurity company.

After some catching up, as we haven't chatted for a while, she started filling me in on some of the issues she was having in her organization:

- "People were having breakfast for too long..." She sighed.

" ...They keep talking and eating and talking, as more people are joining. Last Monday, I counted 8 people sitting for 30 minutes to eat breakfast. This is 4 developers' hours going to waste! How do you suggest I'll make them shorten their breakfast?!" She paused, as it was unclear if she wanted to ask a question or tell a story.

I immediately started thinking on ways she can stop the long gatherings without becoming the bad big boss ruining the party. I came up with several suggestions - like joining herself to breakfast, and after 10 minutes, standing up and saying "thank you all for a magical breakfast... It was great! Now, let's go to work" hoping that the crowd will follow her lead.

Another solution I thought of was to talk with one of the people that is part of the breakfast club - in a private conversation, or during the one-on-one routines - and explaining to her the problematic part of that behavior and so on so forth.

I gave her more and more options.

"Wow! This is great, Gal. I really like it..." she said.

Only after the conversation had ended, and my mind started drifting, I realized I was just plain wrong....

I called her back and (almost) shouted through the car speakers:

"What the hell do I care how long people are eating breakfast for?

Is a long breakfast taboo? Is lunch okay? What about a cigarette break? What about going home at 3:30 PM to pick up the kids? What about working from home? What about playing FIFA in the PlayStation console in the gaming room? Is it okay to get Facebook feed updates? Can I listen to Beyoncé? What about chatting on WhatsApp? What about playing digger or reading tweets" I was out of breath trying to say everything I had in mind while she interrupted me.

"OK, OK, hold your horses. I got the picture. You have a point, I guess. Let me think about it...".

As managers we can't, and more importantly should not, tell people how to spend their time. We should not check when they are coming in the morning or when they are leaving in the afternoon. We should avoid inspecting what they are doing right now.

We should only care about their output, their results, their impact.

As managers, we should make sure the teams and the individuals have enough impactful, interesting, and important things to do.

If we feel (measuring it would be better, but it's not a must) that a team or an individual is underperforming, we should talk about it with them. Vice versa, if they are really talented and do the work of three engineers in half the time, and they are spending the rest of their time playing soccer, we should be happy. We should also make sure they have more challenging work to do.

Lastly, we should make sure that they are appreciated for their job and compensated accordingly; if they will understand that their compensation is related to their output, they will be more motivated and more satisfied.

Don't be bothered by the amount of time people spend eating breakfast. Only care about output and impact.

TIP: Keep a 6:1 positive/negative feedback ratio

Positive feedback is crucial to keep people's motivation high. Research shows that effective relationships in general, and in teams specifically, are in the habit of giving to each other 5.6 positive feedback on each 1 negative one. My favorite example can be found in an article posted by the Harvard Business Review: *The Ideal Praise-to-Criticism Ratio*, by Jack Zenger and Joseph Folkman, back on March 15, 2013

Positive feedback becomes even more important if you are consistent - as you must be - with giving negative (constructive) feedback. **The positive feedback is the gasoline for the person to move forward**

even when they are going up the hill trying to improve on some negative feedback given to them.

I remember that once, in a previous position, I noticed that I was not giving enough positive feedback to the engineers in my team. Once I noticed it, it just stayed in mind, and I acted to change it. Or, at least, tried to change it.

But it wasn't easy. And it came as rather shocking to me, since theoretically, giving positive feedback should be easy, simple, and even fun.

When I've thought about it more, I come to realize that on the one hand, I have very high standards. On the other hand, the team does not meet these standards.

It was one of those '*Ah-ha*' moments that hit you with a thunder sound... After the shock had passed, I decided that this is against my beliefs and I'd taken a series of steps to have a better team, such a team that it would be easy, simple, and fun to give a lot of positive feedback to. Without telling the entire story, I'll just say that after a while, some of the team members were able to meet the expectations, and some didn't (and left the team), while others joined.

However, to my surprise, I noticed that even with a team I considered to be highly skilled, talented, and motivated, still I didn't give them enough positive feedback. Now, I could not blame it on my standards, nor on the team - they were doing great. So why can't I give them positive feedback?

Obviously, once I've thought about it, I could not stop thinking about it, but still moving from thinking on the need to do it, to actually doing it in practice turned out to be not trivial. Though the need to give positive feedback was in my consciousness, the muscle of doing that wasn't trained.

Why is this so hard? It is hard since it is not enough to give someone the thumbs up, or even say "good job!", "Kudos", or "awesome".

I don't consider this to be a professional positive feedback. Actually, if you do it too much, you will soon notice how this becomes meaningless.

Pretty soon, each feature release will be followed by an "Awesome work team!" and then another manager will 'reply all' to the mail thread with "great work!!" and so on and so forth. Not long later, people will be too lazy and will just reply all with +1 or just an icon of thumbs up 👍 .

This will move your organization's culture to be "awesome" but meaningless.

Effective positive feedback should be concrete, specific, and cannot be copy pasted from one person to another one. For example: Dona - I really admire how you have sweated the details on this unit test, it is very important that we keep our tests coverage high.

You see - you cannot copy paste this feedback to another scenario; it's specific to the act Dona did, and it describes exactly what it is that you loved about it.

It's important to do it that way so they can relate to it in their future acts. For example, when they are in a new project and they need to make a decision, whether to write some unit test or not - the fact that their memory is burned with the positive feedback on sweating the details, increases the chance that they will make similar decision in that case as well.

TIP: Help people to utilize their strengths

Though feedback is very important, be careful not to overdo it. Great organizations and wonderful managers know how to give feedback to the people in the team; but they also know how to help the team hide the stuff that are not great and light the stuff that are amazing. They are doing that by staffing the right people on the right tasks, and by using the fact that we are a team and not just a group of individuals.

TIP for the seasoned leader: Hire and Fire

Hiring is the most important thing you have to do. The reason this is so crucial is that this builds the DNA of your team. Any mistake on that, getting the wrong person, might have a tremendous effect on your team's culture. You can see I use hiring all the time in this book as a repeating example since this is so important. For example look in the part on shaping your team's culture via hiring.

The complement of the hiring process is the firing one. Though much more unpleasant also with critical importance. I won't go into too many details on that, in this book, I'd say it has equal importance to hiring, when it comes to keeping your team healthy. If you've exhausted your work with a person in the team on their performance; if you feel there is absolutely nothing more you can do to improve their work, their motivation, or their output, it is time to let go. I would focus on 3 things:

1. Make sure you have done your role to position the person correctly before going into fire them.

2. If you wait too long, you are not helping your team, or the person. On the contrary, it sends the wrong message to the team. A seasoned leader can identify the no return point.

3. Of course, that it's better to have the company and the employee reach an alignment on the need for separation, but if that's not the case, don't drag. Cut it. It's fairer to all parties.

WHEN AND HOW DO YOU NEED TO WORK ON IMPROVING YOUR TEAM?

You need to help people grow all the time. Remember, this is the most important part of your role as a manager.

At best you should give feedback to the members of your team, right after they have done an action that requires feedback. So, if they have conducted a non-efficient meeting, you should give feedback right after it. If their code was thoroughly tested, let them know once you are reviewing it, and so on and so forth.

This should not be done as a "once a year development plan" – it should be done constantly, on the day-to-day job, and on dedicated meetings which usually are named "one-on-one".

TIP: "1:1" meetings are mandatory

Have a constant weekly 1:1 with the people you manage directly, and a monthly meeting with the people you are managing indirectly (i.e., you have a team leader that manages them; these are called skip level meetings).

I've been asked a lot by other managers if it is okay to skip these meetings if you are really busy with other stuff. NO! This is not okay to skip "1-on-1" meetings. This is what you need to do. You need to spend time with the people in the team. This is the job. This is the first priority.

The rest? The rest can follow or can be delegated.

Are you convinced? Go to chapter 8 to get tips and tools on how to perform a perfect 1:1 meeting.

TIP: Trust is the cornerstone for a healthy team

There would be times when you will have to make decisions that are trusted on the input of your team. I think the strongest example here is when you need to hire new developers.

If you are an engineering manager or even the VP of R&D of a small startup, it is probably a good call for you to ask software developer candidates technical questions. Thus, when you need to make the hire/no-hire decisions you have a good context.

But, when you are working on a larger scale organization, specifically if this organization has already a very structured and oriented hiring process - like the one Facebook, Google, or Dropbox practicing - it wouldn't be scalable for you to participate in all the technical interviews of candidates.

In addition, if you are a Director of Engineering or a VP there's a good chance, you'll need to hire software engineers that are specialized in areas you are not an expert in. For example, if you are adding a new front-end team and need a Javascript specialist, or you are establishing a new data science group for the first time.

Lastly, if you are on the higher management, from ROI perspective you'll probably be more fruitful asking all around soft skills questions and check for culture fit/add. Still, you are hiring a software developer, and you need to find out if he has high enough technical bars.

The way to achieve it is by following this easy to understand and hard to accomplish 3-steps rules.

First of all, you need to set up the right hiring process: How to create the pipeline? Interview loop - what should be accomplished and how? How do we decide? Committee, debrief, one-man show? Is a single review enough to decline? The answers to all of these questions vary according to your organization culture, company size, and your own style.

The second step is to train your interviewers and calibrate them: set the expectations, on what to achieve from an interview and also how to do it; once in a while make sure that you and all the interviewers are aligned and calibrated. You can achieve this calibration, by doing one of the following: join as a shadow to an interview, or create a calibration meeting, in which people talk about their last interview, and you get a chance to validate their thinking methods.

The last step is to trust your interviewers: this is the hardest part, but you need to let go. If your interviewer says no, respect it. Trust their opinion; If you don't trust your interviewer, you have a problem:

Either you chose the wrong interviewer, or your interviewer is not trained or calibrated.

You should fix that, but until then, trust your interviewer.

Hiring is an example of how you should **trust the team.**

There are others.

The important thing is to create a safe culture. Safe for people to speak up, to give feedback, to criticize, to improve, to claim mistakes and not to blame others, to fail.

Achieving that is a must. The rest will follow.

Exercise: Feedback

0. On a piece of paper create the following table.

Name	Positive feedback 1	Positive feedback 2	Positive feedback 3	Positive feedback 4	Positive feedback 5	Constuctive feedback
Name 1						
Name 2						
Name 3						
Name 4						
...						

1. In the next couple of weeks, make sure to fill out the table.

2. Don't be afraid to nitpick, good or bad, when you fill it. It can be small or big, technical or on soft skills, anything. Just make sure that it is on a specific behavior you've seen in the last couple of weeks.

3. If you couldn't spot enough points, you should ask yourself why? Maybe you are not close enough to the work? Perhaps you are not included in the right meetings? Might be that you are overloaded with work and didn't have enough time to look at some papers? Maybe people don't feel enough trust with you to share their feelings in the team?

4. Don't deliver this feedback as a whole. This is not the point. The point here was to adjust your mind to think in "feedback". This is your main job; you should train your mind to do it.

5. Obviously, you need to communicate the feedback to your team, but this is a different exercise.

3 KEY TAKEAWAYS

- People, People, People. This should be the number one focus in your management role. Do that first. The rest can wait.

- When people are in their zone, flowing, they are happy. They feel good. Flow can be achieved if they can master their craft. You need to help them to do that. Give them feedback, make them better.

- When people are out of their comfort zone, they are growing. Great developers would like to grow a lot. Coach them, mentor them, challenge them.

Chapter 4

cUlture and Process - the stuff that fuels or kills organizations

WHEN IN DOUBT, THINK CULTURE! THE SECRET OF TURNING A GOOD COMPANY INTO A GREAT ONE...

THE *U* AND *P* OF THE PUPPET PRINCIPLES FOR MANAGERS - 30 MINUTES READ (ADVANCED MATERIAL)

*O*ne of my favorite talks to present in developers conferences is the "zero bugs policy" talk. The long version of it can be found in an article I wrote for the _infoQ magazine_ (published in 2016, April 5th).

The short version is that back in the days when I was working for VMware, we were practicing Scrum to perfection; when it was still considered to be the new bad boy in the neighborhood.

Scrum is just another methodology to implement agile workflows in software development organizations.

*In its essence, one of Scrum's (and agile in general) biggest values is the way it pushes the organization to high quality deliverables. The thing about Scrum though, is that if applied as it written in the books, it pushes the team to keep high quality for **new** code and features, but does not supply rules or guidelines for maintaining high-quality for legacy products; nor how to handle customers issues reported from the field.*

There are other more suitable agile implementations that give better guidelines for handling customer issues (like Kanban or Scrumban), but we won't get into these in this book.

Going back to our story on the "zero bugs policy"...

In VMware, since we have developed mainly enterprise-grade products, the quality had to be top-notch. Not just for the new features we've been developing, but also for bugs found later in the game.

The fact of the matter was, however, that our processes were tuned into keeping high quality for newly developed features, but not for handling bugs reported by the customers on products already running in the field.

After a lot of trials and errors to our processes, I invented back in 2012 a new bugs handling process and named it - "the zero bugs policy".

It is a manifesto on how to triage and manage bugs. The manifesto states that you shouldn't manage bugs at all. Instead, for each new bug that is reported, you should either **fix** the bug immediately (at least in the next couple of weeks) **or close** it as 'won't fix' - and never think about it again. Thus, you are not adding more and more bugs to your backlog and preventing a triage nightmare.

After implementing the policy successfully in the local Israeli site, the "zero bugs policy" started spreading to other GEOs in VMware as well.

At the same time, I started socializing the idea in development conferences and relevant meetups.

By the end of 2018, it was already implemented by a few large corporations and several startups. I even heard of a new tool that helps companies follow the policy.

Towards the end of the "zero bugs policy" talk, I'm referring to one of the agile principles I like most from the agile manifesto. By the way, if you are not familiar with the agile manifesto, you should really grab your favorite coffee and 2 hours on the sofa and get acquainted with <u>it</u> - <u>The Agile Manifesto</u>.

Basically, the agile manifesto is the bible for agile development, written in the early millennium by an elite group of 15 senior software personas, like Martin Fowler, Uncle Bob Martin, and others. It describes the changes that need to be done in the way we create software.

There are several principles in the agile manifesto, but the one I refer to in this context is: **"prefer people and interactions over processes and tools."**

The reason I love this principle is that it holds an inherent conflict.

Scrum, for example, is a way to implement agile. But it is a process as much as a process can be. It has rules and ceremonies, tools and roles.

But the agile manifesto implies that we should not default to processes and tools.

How can this quandary be resolved?

I think this is the beautiful thing about Scrum - though at first, it requires you to follow a very well-structured process; pretty soon, if applied correctly with the right amount of patience and attitude, it turns the entire way your company behaves and thinks. It is a cultural game changer.

The "zero bugs policy" has the same nature. At first, it starts as a rigid process, but given enough time and the right attitude, it would change the entire way your company is approaching quality and decision making.

There are a few more interesting learnings you can take from the "zero bugs policy" - on processes, quality, culture and adopting changes.

LEAN & CRISP PROCESSES ARE THE RAIL TRACK THE COMPANY IS RIDING ON

WHAT IS A PROCESS?

A process is a series of actions or steps taken in order to achieve a particular end.

Companies must have processes in order for them to operate.

Even a simple thing like scheduling a meeting is a process - you have several steps you need to take in order to achieve your goal. In that case, the goal is a meeting.

Let's see what naive steps needed in order to schedule a meeting:

1. Come up with a meeting's subject.

2. Decide on the meeting's participants. Maybe some of them are mandatory and some of them are optional.

3. Decide on the meeting's agenda.

4. Decide on the meeting's length based on the agenda.

5. Decide on the time of the meeting based on its length and participants availability.

6. Decide on the location of the meeting based on all of the above parameters.

7. Send a meeting invite to the relevant participants.

8. Get confirmation from participants that they can and want to join.

And so on and so forth.

Eight steps. This is a process of creating a meeting.

Maybe in some organizations, the process of creating meetings is different. In Google, for example, all the meetings are either 25 minutes or 50 minutes (it means that step 4 should be refined a bit). The idea is to leave 5/10 minutes to get organized before the next meeting starts, in order to avoid meeting delays.

Some companies do not allow optional people to be invited to a meeting. The idea is that people should either attend or not. You should not overcrowd a meeting with people that are not mandatory, nor should you waste their time.

In Dropbox for example, some of the engineering groups hold a "no meeting Wednesday" rule; this means that people are not scheduling meetings for Wednesday. The idea is to allow at least 1 day of the week that is with zero interruptions and allow "makers" to have dedicated time without context switches. So they can get to the zone.

Some companies do not allow meetings at all. Or at least no routine meetings, or meetings that are not with just 2 participants.

Each one of the examples above is a process. Even a "no process" is a process. It defines exactly what to do or what not to do.

Some of the processes above are heavy and cumbersome, and some are crisp and elegant. Some might be a good fit for some companies, and some might not fit at all. It really depends on the company's DNA.

The most important thing about a healthy process is to constantly keep checking whether the process is indeed required and if it's as crisp as it could be. **You always need to have a thread in the back of your mind, going over all the processes in your team, asking if a process can be shorter, simpler, or more elegant.** Is the process' result as good as you wish, and what are the negative side effects it might have?

In my early days as a team leader and even later on as a Junior engineering manager, a top-notch process was my default answer whenever I've stumbled into an area that was not functioning as smoothly as I expected:

The build keeps failing, either due to failed tests, or due to bad integration, or to wrong deployment configuration - that is easy, let's create a process for that. We will have an on-call duty rotation. Each week we will have a dedicated engineer responsible for the build's health and jumping to fix it once it breaks.

We don't have enough "knowledge sharing" in the team - worry not! Each Tuesday another person would be in charge of sharing their knowledge with the rest of the team. This person would create a dedicated wiki section and spend half an hour presenting it to the team.

We are not innovative enough – rest your mind! let's create a VIIF - VMware Israeli innovation festival. It will be a 2 days event. We will create ad-hoc teams of 4 developers, each team will have a demo, 5 judges will decide who is the most innovative project... There will be prizes!

All of the above examples actually happened. Also, they have all improved our software organization. Processes are good. When processes are done correctly, they are what make an organization pace the right way.

However, without the required grain of salt, processes might be the thing that reduces the effectiveness of the team and in time will softly kill your organization.

THE VALUE OF VALUES

"Around the beginning of 2017, I got invited to a closed social community group. It was dedicated to R&D leaders. One of the first questions raised by the group's owner, who has been a newbie team leader, was "In hindsight, what would you have liked to know when you first became a team leader?"

My answer was that in my first years as a manager I always ran away to process everything. I'd done that because I was good at it, and it was easy. Creating a process, and executing it well falls right into the comfort zone of first-time software managers. Why?

First, because processes that applied correctly have a high return on investment (ROI), at least for the short-term.

It's fulfilling, satisfying even.

Just like writing a few lines of code, compiling them, running the program and see your application running on the screen. Yay!

Second, because creating a process has similarities to writing code; defining a process is just like writing a flow chart.

It took me quite a while before I realized processing should be the last resort.

As I've written above - **good lean processes are essential to keep the organization running.**

Unfortunately, though, **processes can also be evil**.

First of all, too many processes or processes that feel too tight or too loose, can quickly create an atmosphere of bureaucracy in a large corporation. We will see an example of that in the next page.

If people in your organization are complaining that the company is drifting to bureaucracy, I urge you to go ahead and try to drill down to why do they feel that way. Ask them to give you 4 reasons.

I bet a cup of good coffee, that they will answer the following in this exact order:

1. Too many emails.

2. Too many meetings.

3. Too many processes.

4. Paralysis analysis (or some other formation of bad/slow decision making).

I believe that this would be the order since the first couple of answers - emails and meetings - are the two issues engineers commonly complain about. It's just always on their top complaints list. It makes sense, since engineers want to write code, or to design a system. Anything else is considered waste.

The third one - processes - requires a bit more inner digging to get and the fourth one (decisions) is the most complicated one to observe. Also, in some cases, the slow decision-making is the result of too many processes.

Bureaucracy and slowness are not the only evils for processing everything. The real problem is that processes by nature are specific and can't cover everything.

Let's consider the following "back to the future" example that illustrates both how processes can create bureaucracy and why they are just not enough.

BACK TO THE FUTURE EXAMPLE

In the last retrospective meeting - this is the meeting where the team reflects back on the last few weeks in order to continuously improve their work - the team said that they feel the quality of the code and processes do not have high enough standards to support the current scale of the product. Since the product is already being used by millions of users, this is a huge potential risk.

As a mitigation, they suggested a couple of paradigms we should follow from now on.

First, each code change (a diff) will be reviewed by at least two developers before it can be pushed to production (landed).

Second, the automation tests will cover at least 95% lines of code (or similar, more function-based metrics if you prefer).

The team is happy!

After just a few weeks the quality has improved. The code has improved and there were fewer bugs found by the quality assurance team (QA). Yay!

This is what's so great about processes, when they are working - you can see their value promptly.

Jumping 3 weeks into the future, people in the team have started complaining...

"Why do I need to slow down my progress?! Waiting for 2 reviewers to find the time to review and approve my diff... Just for a stupid string change?"

"This is a damn POJO (Plain Old Java Object) class - 95% testing coverage for that really worth the ROI (Return of Investment)?"

The team level of frustration went up. Slowly, but steadily. Generally speaking, sometimes the frustration is real, occasionally it is just "birth pangs".

When you think about it, these types of processes, by design, are slowing down the progress of the team.

Jumping 3 more weeks into the future, a new quandary has arisen.

There was a bug reported by one of our largest customers.

The team didn't know if they should stop everything and fix the bug right now, or they should just continue developing their super important feature, which will bring new value to our entire market.

The processes the team had come up with before - mandating double code reviews and retaining high testing coverage - did not help this specific case.

So, a new process needed to be invented. Maybe a good idea would be to have some kind of bug court - this is a weekly meeting of stakeholders that are going over all the bugs and deciding their priorities and the required action items to take on them accordingly. Maybe we need a new role, a Chief of Quality that would be responsible for such issues.

And so on and so forth.

Now, let's go back in time again. 2-3 months before, just when the team felt there is a quality risk that needed to be addressed. Right before all the new and shiny processes were introduced, to begin with.

An alternative approach was to ask a higher-level question.

What do we think about quality? Is top quality a meaningful value for our company? Do we really care about it or is it more of a temporal, even tentative state?

Is quality always more important to our team than other things (like velocity, or innovation or whatnot)?

If it is a big thing, a value we want to nurture - **let's say it.** Let's define "top quality" or "quality comes first" as a leading value for us.

If it is not, if it's just a breeze - we need to think if we'd like to invest time in creating shiny processes that by definition would be short-termed, or we should just breeze through that temporary phase.

Assuming we've defined quality as a top value - how does it come into play?

First of all, the developers are not forced into 2 reviews on each code change. Alternatively, each time they are going into an inner debate - whether to ask for one review or two reviews, three reviews or even just push it to production without any review at all - they will turn to the value and it will guide them to the right decision.

Same goes with the testing coverage. It's under the empowerment and the ownership of the developers to decide if the current line of code requires manual validation, unit testing, integration testing or no testing at all. We trust their judgment, but we do give them guidelines. We give them a lighthouse to light their path. This is the value of "quality comes first". We've eliminated process and gained empowerment and sense of ownership.

But wait! You haven't heard the coolest thing yet!

Now, when the new quality problem will arise, whether to fix a bug that was found in the field during our current sprint or to continue with implementing the feature, we are now working on - Of course we should fix it! Hey, "Quality comes first".

We have a value to lead us, and we don't need to invent a shiny new process.

Back to the future example - The end (-;

I'd like to mention a tiny disclaimer to the above. By all means, I don't believe that the entire company culture can or should be based on a small set of defined and explicit values. It is quite natural and makes sense that at least some of them would be more implicit.

For example, even if we don't have "extreme visibility" as a value on the wall, we can still have extreme visibility as part of our culture. Actions matters. So, if we are having frequent all-hands meetings where we share the company status, and we allow people to ask live questions, and the walls of the meeting rooms are made from glass so it can be seen through, we are on the way to having a visible culture.

Uri Nativ, VP R&D, Torii, is one of my previous managers. He was the one who taught me how to mentally think about developing an organization culture.

Once I heard a talk from Uri where he said: *"when in doubt - think culture; you can delegate the rest".* You can find it here.

I think that this short sentence holds inside of it the bare essence of this chapter. As a manager, you need to focus your time on building the right culture for your team. This is very important, because it will define the way your team behaves, and through that, the way your team operates.

THE PRACTICE - HOW TO TURN VALUES FROM A POSTER ON THE WALL TO THE COMPANY'S DNA?

It's really hard and complicated to build a well-established great culture.

There are tons of books, posts, and podcasts about it, and by all means, it's a matter for a different book.

However, there are some basic rules, guidelines, and tips for building and maintaining a great culture. In this book, I'm focusing on the cultural aspects that a manager/leader needs to take into account, and not on the organization as a whole.

TIP: start with the process and transform it into a culture

Especially for junior managers, since it is much easier to think about the process than culture, don't fight with that too much. You can start with the process and once comfortable, transform it into a culture.

Let's assume for example you'd like to create a culture of continuous improvement in your team. It's a bit vague, right? I mean, where do you even start? It starts by improving your product and quality, via having your people aiming higher and doing self-improvement and goes all the way through improving your processes and tools.

It takes time until the DNA of a software team levels up to that extent.

As a rule of thumb, people in general and software developers, in particular, are not big fans of changes. Asking them to constantly change is radical.

So, don't try to boil the ocean in one day. At this point of your career, it is fine you don't have all the answers, as long as you do see the culture shift as the north-star of your direction; so, for now - just start small.

Taking the continuous improvement example, you can have a monthly session of post-mortem to a selected bug. Have your team figure out (and later present to a wider group) what could we have done differently in order to prevent the bug from happening? What could we have done to detect the bug quicker? And what could we have done in order to fix it faster (in hindsight obviously)?

After four or five times of you following this technique, you'll start noticing that people are doing a verbal informal post-mortem to other bugs as well, without you pushing them to do it.

This would be the beginning of the culture shift you had in mind as your north star.

TIP for the junior manager: find your own values

I believe that each manager, whether they are just starting their path in managing people, and definitely if they are well-experienced, should have a set of explicit, well-defined, not too long, list of values.

The list can be adjusted over time but having such a list at all times is a must.

This is the backbone of your management approach. If you don't have such a list, it means you are just improvising as you go.

As we've discussed above, not all the values must be written in bold Helvetica fonts on the walls of the company. Some do. Some can be implicit.

My personal values sum up into 2 main explicit ones: Teamwork & Continuous improvement.

I've thought about these specific values a lot, and for me, they are more than just words on a paper. I think that in the beginning of my career as a people manager they were not even my main values. It was a long time ago, but I believe it was something around responsibility, independence, and looking at the big picture. Overwhelming to think how much they have changed; how much have I changed.

Team work and continuous improvement.

In a nutshell, teamwork is not just the ability of members in the team to drink beer/coffee together. That too. And it's not just about being nice. That too. As Netflix stated it accurately: *"we don't hire brilliant jerks"*.

It's mainly about the understanding that the team's tasks are more important than my own tasks. Followed by the willingness to put in the time, and energy in order to progress the team's tasks, even if my commitments would get delayed.

Also, it's the ability of the team members to give feedback to one another, in a helpful, respectful, and trusted way. Just like the wonderful research by Google, showing that effective teams are the ones that are able to create a safe zone in the team.

The safe zone creates an atmosphere where teammates feel they can speak up without being afraid of fallouts. In such a trusted environment, people can give feedback to each other, thus people in the team can improve the performance of themselves and of the team much faster; people can come up with creative ideas, without the feeling that they will be handled disrespectfully, and so on. See for reference Google's Five Keys to a Successful Google Team.

This brings us straight to my personal second value - continuous improvement.

I consider this value as the fuel of the organization. When it exists, it pushes the product to be finer, it purifies the process to be adequate, it encourages the team to try and use state-of-the-art technologies, and it motivates the people to improve.

Another terminology for continuous improvement is coming from Japan - The Toyota System, which is probably one of the biggest influencers on the way agile software development is done today. The Toyota system uses the term **Kaizen** which is "improvement" in Japanese. *It also applies to processes, such as purchasing and* logistics, *that cross organizational boundaries into the* supply chain.[1] *It has been applied in* healthcare,[2] psychotherapy,[3] life-coaching, *government, banking, and other industries. By improving standardized programs and processes, kaizen aims to eliminate waste (see* lean manufacturing). (<u>Wikipedia, Kaizen</u>)

If you are working in a top-notch company, people that are standing still are actually moving back...and only if you move forward you are able to keep up the pace.

TIP for the startup leader: Choose your values carefully, but don't fall in love with them

If you are starting/joining a startup you should choose your values carefully.

You are going to invest a lot of time making sure that your values are not just a poster on the wall. That they become the DNA of the company.

You are going to use these values for making decisions.

Hence, you better choose the right values.

You better **make sure that your values would not contradict each other**. If they will be contradicting, they will lose any meaning, since they won't be your north star, they won't be your campus or your balance during challenging crossroads.

For example, let's assume you are a small startup aimed at the consumer market and you are inventing a new application for a beauty product. This type of industry nurtures the express trend and the constant innovation - you probably want to make sure you have a value that talks about the speed of iteration or high delivery pace or short feedback loop.

So far, so good.

But if one of the values you already defined is for "sweating the details", or "quality comes first", you are fooling yourself. You can't really have it all, not for the long-term, not consistently.

In this case for example, if you move fast, things break. You should accept that. You cannot have it both ways.

The opposite example is a startup that has already grown and has moved from selling to consumers (end users), into selling to enterprise companies which are selling beauty products. Now, high quality is probably more important than delivering 5 new innovative features a month. Suddenly, "quality comes first" is more important than "move fast".

So, the bottom line here is to choose the values wisely, but also not to fall in love with them. The values, among other things, should serve the company's mission. If the company's mission has changed, or was even just adjusted, make sure you are checking to see if your values need a refresh as well.

TIP: Hire and measure according to your explicit values

I've learned this one during my time at Dropbox.

Dropbox has a very strong and identified culture. Without going into the exact details of the values constructing this culture, I've learned that one way to make it so strong, is to make them inherent to the hiring process and a cornerstone in your performance evaluating themes.

Just for the sake of the example, let's assume that one of your main values is "We admire endurance - we don't easily give up, we value long-term results and not short-term wins." If endurance is a top value you need to make sure that when you are interviewing people, you get a clear signal for their endurance abilities.

You can ask them for example, what was the longest project in their previous work? How did they feel about it? Was it hard? Was it fun? Did it have phases? How was the collaboration around such a long project?

You can even ask them directly if they prefer a one-year project or three months project...

You should also embed the values into your performance evaluation process.

Following the same example, you need to make sure you celebrate projects that required endurance - since they were very long, or since they had a lot of tiny obstacles during the way.

Also make sure that you put enough time, energy, and focus in working with the employees that are facing endurance challenges - since they tend to show a lot of frustrations when projects are taking forever, or if they get bored quickly, or they just don't have the stamina to pull such a long or hard way.

TIP: Create a language.

Another beautiful thing I saw happening in Dropbox was the way the company embeds the values into its day-to-day language.

For example, one of Dropbox's values back in the days was "sweat the details" which means it is really important to think about all the edge cases and not to leave anything uncovered. This value was so embedded into Dropbox's culture, that it has been part of the terminology people use in their day-to-day communication. You can actually see one developer comment on a code review for a diff of her teammate, something like *'great sweating the details on that one'*. I'm using the past tense since by now, Dropbox decided to drop this value for another that seemed more suitable to its current phase.

Avi Etzioni was my partner in crime for podcasting a Hebrew podcast for software developers. He told me that while he was the VP of R&D of the startup Oribi, they held a similar approach - several of the values they adopted turned into a second language. When things got hard and challenging you could have heard in the open-space of Oribi one developer tells the Product Manager "Let's default to positive".

Embedding the values of the company to its language sometimes happens on its own, but you should help. You need to use your values when appropriate. People will follow. It's your job as a manager to correlate your words and actions with the values.

In Dropbox, for example, when my team had completed a task above and beyond expectations, and I sent them a recognition mail, I signed it with "#aim-higher" which was at the time one of Dropbox core values. This sent a clear message to the team that mapped between their achievement to the value on the wall and encouraging them to pursue the same patterns in the future.

TIP for the director: Organizational structure

One of the most underestimated parameters that impacts the culture of an organization unit is the way it is structured.

Vice versa, the way the company's culture impacts the organization structure; it is undervalued as well.

Since the way to build an organization, and moreover the way to scale it, is a topic big enough to be covered in a separate book, I will only point out here some examples that illustrate the connection between the two, but without diving deep.

Back in the VMware days, I managed a group of 25 developers.

I structured the group in such a way that they were divided into 4 Scrum teams, where each team had a manager.

The manager was responsible for managing the people from talent perspective, and was also the Scrum Master for the team; according to the Scrum theory, the Scrum Master in a team is someone who is responsible for coaching the team on the right Scrum practices. In practice, the Scrum Master spends most of their time on managing the different ceremonies in the Scrum process.

Since I was not managing the engineers directly, de facto we had 1 more layer of management than the absolute must. At some point I felt that this extra layer was slowing us down, and causing some feelings of over-bureaucracy by the developers; my thinking was that each layer of management is an extra layer of decisions approval processes so it made sense that this is the reason I felt we are slower than we potentially could be.

I've started a limited time experiment where the 4 team managers have dropped their manager's hats and have focused only on being Scrum Master and tech leaders.

I personally took over all the stuff related to people management, like talent development, hiring, and such. Even before the experiment, I was highly involved in these topics, both in mentoring the team's managers, but also directly; hence, the overload on me was felt, but not to the point it was unmanageable. At least, so I thought.

After 2 months I shut down the experiment and marked it as a failure.

Why did the experiment fail?

First of all, developers in the team did not get enough feedback, coaching, and mentoring (from me), since I could not scale that way. I thought I could, but turned out I was wrong,

What about moving faster? Well, we had less bureaucracy - since each decision was made faster. This is pure math, if you have fewer management layers, you need fewer approval to reach decisions and occasionally the teams feel more empowered to make decisions themselves.

However, the teams were lacking focus and order; so, in our specific case, the teams may have moved faster, but they didn't move in the right direction.

The point of this story is not to show you how I've tried and failed, though this is a valuable lesson as well. I wanted to demonstrate how the way you are building your team influences your culture. In this case, on the culture of delivery on the one hand, and on talent development from the other.

Hence, you need to remember that each time you are making organization change, it has the potential to impact your culture. Don't be afraid of that, use it to your advantage; if a culture change is needed - good! If not, think if the new organization structure supports the current culture or not.

TIP: decision making - when in doubt turn into your values

This is the chicken and the egg problem, but it's important that once you have set your values, you will turn to them when quandary appears. I've mentioned it above, but I'll repeat since it's very important:

If you don't use your values when you are facing hard choices, then you have the wrong values.

If you don't use your values, when you are making decisions, then your values will just be a poster on the wall.

More on decision making in the last chapter of this book.

MANAGEMENT EXERCISES

Exercise: Fine-tune a process

1. Think about the processes you have in your team, in your group, in your organization.

2. Choose three processes that you have a direct influence on their flow. Write them down: PR0, PR1, PR2.

3. **From these three processes, do the following:**

   3.1. Simplify - choose one of the three processes and make it simpler. Remove one of its phases, delete some of its branches, reduce the number of people that need to interact with it. Make it simpler. Make it more efficient.

   3.2. Delete - choose one of the other two processes and delete them. For a month, declare an experiment in the team. The process is no longer valid, we do not follow it. After a month, check what happened; Did life get better or worse?

   3.3. Culturfy - try to take the 3rd process and think if there is something in your culture, in the company values or in the team values, that already defines (without words) the expected behavior. If so, maybe the process can be eliminated, while we emphasize that part of the culture. If not, and this is an advanced exercise, should we consider some culture change? Is it important enough to be in our values? Start a discussion on that with your team, or with your colleagues.

3 KEY TAKEAWAYS

- Processes are easy to create but are hard to maintain. Too many of them will slowly kill your organization.

- Creating a culture is better than creating a process.

- Don't accept the status quo. Processes need tuning, culture needs revisiting.

Chapter 5

From knowing the Product to understanding the businEss

WHY SHOULD MANAGERS CARE ABOUT THE COMPANY'S MISSION AND GOALS?

THE *P* AND *E* PARTS OF THE PUP*PE*T FRAMEWORK FOR MANAGERS - 24 MINUTES READ

*I*n Dropbox, there is an "all-hands" ceremony for the entire company almost on a bi-weekly cadence.

"All-hands" is a nice phrasing which indicates that all the employees in the organization are invited. Its origin comes from the sailing world, where the captain requires all the sailors to come up to the deck to help navigate the boat in a raging ocean.

Photo by Stijn Swinnen on Unsplash

The entire company is gathered in the tuck shop - Dropbox's famous in-house restaurant in San Francisco - where Dropbox headquarters are located. The remote sites are joined by video conference or by streaming.

Drew Houston is the Dropbox CEO and co-founder. Drew hosts most of the "all-hands" gathering, and usually speaks at least at some portion of it.

Drew speaks about a variety of topics, like the latest changes to the hiring process, the new buildings Dropbox is planning to expand to, Dropbox's success and failures over the last quarter, diversity, equity and inclusion (DEI), the hack week - and a lot more.

The topics are changeable according to the high time of the week.

There is one thing in each all-hands session that is not changeable - almost always, Drew will either mention the Dropbox mission and goals for this year, or will tell a story on some really unique company that is in the business of saving the world, and happens to use Dropbox as one of its main collaboration tools.

In my first months at Dropbox, I valued the visibility that these all-hands meetings give, but I was clueless about the importance of mission and goals that were always highlighted.

WHY SHOULD YOU CARE ABOUT THE PRODUCT?

There are software companies that have a dedicated Product Manager (PM) or a Product Owner (PO). The PM and the PO are the ones that are responsible for defining the production's vision and handling the product roadmap. They need to understand the market and the market fit for the product the company is developing.

There are other companies in which all of these aspects are done by the Engineering Manager and not by a dedicated product persona (PM/PO).

Why? It might be because this is a startup that started from tech/engineering and isn't at scale that needs this yet; it might be because it's a company that is developing very tech-oriented features (a lot of the cybersecurity companies are such), and maybe it's just the way the company chose to operate.

In HubSpot, a company that is developing marketing, sales, and service software, for example, although they do have product managers (PMs), they are encouraging their engineering managers to focus on people and product aspects of the management responsibilities, and not on the process aspect of it. This is just their management philosophy. You can see more about it a blogpost they have published in Medium on April, 17 - *"Why our engineering leaders focus on product over process"*.

Either way and even if in your organization there is a dedicated product manager or a product owner, some accountability of the product lies in the hands of the engineering manager - your hands. I'll try to articulate why.

For example, if you are a director of a large engineering group with 30 people reporting to you, you need to understand what you want to build in order to be able to staff a project correctly.

If you don't understand the product well, you won't be able to know which kind of skills and experience you need to put for this project. If this product has extensive UI screens, you probably need someone that can write front-end. If the product has complicated search capabilities, maybe you need someone who is a database expert or a scale master. Does the product need to support mobile phones? Then you need an iOS developer or an android one or both. Does it have dependencies to other domains you do not own, but you need to collaborate with?

So, it's clear why understanding the product is critical if you are managing a large operation, but even if you manage just 5 people, being a product owner is critical. You need to understand the market, customers and the use cases. If you don't, you will not be able to know what to focus the team's execution on.

Let's assume, for example, you are working in the fin-tech industry. Your company is building a product that serves as the website for banks. Now, the product manager is asking you to do some modifications to the login page. You know that you are developing a product for banks, that means you understand that security comes first. Obviously. You will put the right pressure on building a secured product and focus the testing on penetration tests and so on.

But, if you'll drill further you might be interested to find out that the product is aimed mostly for small banks - that their maximum traction is 10K customers - above that, due to compliance reasons, banks have to create their own systems (I'm making all this up for the sake of illustration). In that case, it means you can focus less on building ultra-scale platform, and more on a very slick user experience.

You need to understand the overall picture. If you don't understand the expectations of the customers of this product, you won't understand the milestones. You need to understand them in order to staff the right team that would be able to deliver it on time. You need to create the right processes in order to meet the quality bar and the expected milestones.

All of these above examples are simplified. Real life is more complicated. But the idea is the same. Product matters.

TIP: EPD collaboration.

Even as a manager, and though it sometimes does not feel like it, you are not alone. The way to succeed is to work together with the other functions in the organization, collaborate with them closely in order to achieve a shared goal.

In companies like Dropbox and Facebook, there are 3 kind of functions that work closely together on each project. They are referred to as EPD - engineering, product, and design.

You need to invest time and energy to build trusting relationships with your product manager, and UX designer peers. Once you all work together, with a full alignment, and open communication channels, the entire organization would be much more effective.

WHY SHOULD YOU CARE ABOUT THE MISSION AND GOALS?

Great companies - or more accurately, great people who are running great companies - invest heavily in defining the mission of their organization.

If you happen to meet such successful CEOs, they will tell you how they spent months thinking on the right mission for their company. Then they spent weeks in order to refine the mission. Eventually, they reviewed it with others, thinking about each word, their order, their meaning, and non-meaning. The same process of missioning should and does also happen in subsections of the company.

What is a mission? A **company's mission** is a unified aspiration that articulates why a company exists, what it offers, and how the world will be a better place as a result.

Google, for example, defined their mission in the following way:

Our mission is to organize the world's information and make it universally accessible and useful.

As you can see, they didn't say that they are building a search engine or a mailing server. Their mission is much bigger. It's about the world, the universe.

Now, each year (at least) Google and similar companies would create a set of goals in order to get them a bit closer to their mission. What are company business goals? **Business goals** describe what a **company** expects to accomplish over a specific period of time. Usually, a company breaks down the mission into a set of 3-5 business goals that need to be achieved in the upcoming year. Meeting these goals would move the company closer towards fulfilling its mission.

Going back to our example. Google has several divisions. Each division has a different goal. You can think about it as a sub-mission. Completing the goal (or sub-mission) by a division would bring Google closer to achieving its mission.

A goal might be developing the next generation of a search engine based on AI. It can also be business-related, like increasing the number of users or sales related like 10% up in ARR (Annual Recurring Revenue) or it can even be related to hiring - have 50% women engineers - if the company believes it would help its mission, and so on and so forth.

Companies tend to put in place all kinds of methodologies, frameworks, and tools in order to track and grade their progress in accomplishing their goals.

One such method that is commonly used by leading companies like Google and Dropbox is called OKR.

*"**Objectives and Key Results** (OKR) is a framework for defining and tracking objectives and their outcomes.*

The OKR framework was created by Intel CEO Andy Grove and brought to Google by venture capitalist John Doerr and has been used by several companies including Google, LinkedIn, Twitter and Uber.

The OKR framework aims to define a company's and team's "objectives" along with linked and measurable "key results" to provide "a critical thinking framework and ongoing discipline that seeks to ensure employees work together, focusing their efforts to make measurable contributions."[7] OKRs are typically set at the company, team and personal levels and may be shared across the organization with the intention of providing teams with visibility of goals with the intention to align and focus effort." (Wikipedia: OKR)

It seems kind of straightforward to understand why companies and CEOs put so much time and energy into missions and goals. **But why should the engineering managers care so much about them?**

Why are the business landscape, the mission, and the goals of the company for this year so important?

Is it in order for the engineers to be able to develop products that are a good fit for the requirements and customer's needs? Well, yes of course, but that is not the main thing.

Is it in order for the developers to be able to innovate based on understanding the market shape and competition portfolio? Well, yes but that is not the only reason.

Is it in order to make sure that the engineers understand the priorities so they will focus only on the most important things? Well, this is crucial, but there are more methodical ways to accomplish that.

In order to deeply understand the importance of the mission and business goals, let's have a close look at the following anecdote:

Dropbox and VMware - two companies I got to know quite deeply - use to run an employee satisfaction survey. It is an anonymous form, that was sent to all the employees each quarter or so.

All the employees in the company answer an identical set of questions that can indicate some of the satisfaction metrics for employees. Actually, this practice is common in most of the companies that shifted up from the startup scale and care deeply about their employees' satisfaction. Some examples of typical questions might be:

- How happy are you working for Dropbox?

- Do you feel connected to Google's brand?

- Do you think you will be working for VMware 1 year from now?

Well, this makes sense. What's more surprising is that one of the questions in these surveys is: **"Do you understand the company's goals?"**

You must be wondering, how is the answer to that question a good indication of the employee's satisfaction?

It took me a while to understand the importance of this as a manager. On the one hand it sounds trivial, right? You should be familiar with the business you are in and the product you are working on, but that, in my opinion, isn't the main point.

The main point is to connect your team to the company's mission and goals. Now wait, I know, this sounds like the kitschiest thing ever, and to some extent it is.

Mission and goals are important for all of the reasons above, but mainly they are important in order to have or to feel a sense of **purpose**.

Going back to Daniel Pink's book on motivation and drive, one of the most surprising findings to me of his research was the importance of the purpose factor into one's inner motivation and drive.

Apparently, knowledge workers that are working on technical challenging problems, care about doing it for a purpose. They would like to be proud of their work. They would like to tell their family and friends what they are doing and to take pride in that. They would like to change the world or at least have a meaningful impact on it.

The fact of the matter is that most of us are **not** working on products that help decrease world poverty or save kittens in need. But, still, we are creating something meaningful that makes a change (otherwise we wouldn't have done that).

Thus, in order for us to feel proud of our work, **to have a purpose**, we need to understand how the things we are doing day-to-day are part of our department's goals, and how are these, contribute to the company's mission.

We must believe that what we are doing is different or better than the competitors...Since if we are all doing the same thing, what is the **purpose** of doing it?

For our day-to-day tasks, challenges, interest, autonomy, and mastery might be enough, but for us to drive a long road we must need a purpose, a meaning.

APPLYING THE DYNAMIC OF THE PUPPET PRINCIPLES

The PUPPET (People, cUlture, Process, Product, businEss, Technology) principles are dynamic. Let's see how it comes to play here.

As **Junior Engineering Manager** you should probably focus on the features and product level. It is your responsibility to make sure you understand the product surface areas in order to implement the right things the right way. Remember the simple banking application example from above - if you don't really understand the type of customers you are aiming to satisfy, and if you don't fully understand the product vision you cannot decide on the right trade-offs: quality versus speed, scale versus simplicity, security versus UX, and so on and so forth.

It should be on your order of business to get a deeper understanding of the company goals, and business landscape, but since this is not part of your day-to-day, it will consume a lot of energy to understand the strategy of that. I would treat this as a growth opportunity. This would probably be something out of your comfort zone. It would be one of these things that are nice add-ons, but not mandatory **for now**.

If you are a second line manager, **Director in a large company or the VP of R&D** of a startup you should be able to articulate to the engineering team the market needs, how the goals you have set up are mapped to the company vision and mission, and also how the work that the team will do in the next iteration is mapped to that.

In either role, you don't have tons of opportunities to do it, so you need to use the ones you have fully. It should come up in 1-on-1 meetings at least on a monthly basis, it should come up when you are doing an all-hands meeting or a weekly "state of the union" meeting with your group.

Mostly, you need to make the connection when it is clear. For example, when a new feature launched, congratulating the team is only part of the job, you also need to connect this release to the company's goals. You will see an example on how to do that in the tips section below.

THE PRACTICE - HOW TO EMBED THE MISSION AND GOALS?

TIP: State, explain, repeat

- The recipe is simple. But it requires persistence.

- State the vision/mission.

- State the goals; explain how the goals map to the vision.

- State the day-to-day tasks; explain how these are mapped to the goals.

- Repeat forever.

The thing about goals and mission: even if they are super clear and articulated, and even if you do connect the dots between them to the day-to-day work, they still seem like a cloud in the sky. So far away; abstract. You can never really reach them.

This is why as a manager you need to work twice as hard in order to bring them to life.

I remember a time when my entire team worked on features that had direct links to the company goals. **Moreover**, I spent at least 10 minutes in each in 1-on-1 meetings with the developers talking with them about the company goals. But still, when the quarterly satisfaction survey came we got a very low score on the question: "I understand how my work relates to the company's goals."

I was surprised and disappointed, so I approached my team and asked them about it. It turned out that though it was crystal clear to me, it wasn't clear for my team. The link from the day-to-day tasks to the company's goals was vague at best. They understood the company's goals. Some of them even liked them. They just could not see a direct link to the stuff they were working on.

After some thought and brainstorming, we decided to create an online rolling paper that captures at all time a relation between the tasks people are doing, and the company's goals. That way, all the people in the team have a clear updated understanding of the line between their work and the company's goals.

After doing it for a couple of months, I saw an increase to the score of that question by 20%. But that is not the point. The point was that now people had a sense of purpose. And a sense of purpose creates a drive. Moreover, the byproduct was that we spotted several tasks that were not linked to the goals, not even remotely. We've eliminated them. Stayed focused on the important things first.

TIP for the manager: Divide into big rocks

The reality is that a lot of the time, our team is not currently focused on building the *next BIG thing*. Sometimes our engineers are occupied with tons of small tasks, pesky asks, and maintenance work.

Assuming you are positive that these tasks are actually needed, your manager role here is to think hard on how to package the work of your team in such a way that it would mean something.

It might be a weird exercise at first which might even look like "just for perception" kind of act, but if putting in the right mind and energy to do that, you'll end up with one of two positive outcomes.

Either you will be able to bucket the things into large enough boxes, which will give your team a sense of purpose, or you'll find out that you just are not focusing on the things that are important to the company's mission and you need to change direction.

Let's take a look at a few easy and simplified examples.

Instead of talking about "extracting some code from the monolith", you can talk about "microservices architecture in order to allow scalability, agility, and fast development for future roadmap".

Instead of talking about "refactoring for class A of some sort", you should frame it as "foundation work in order to improve the code quality".

TIP for the Director: storytelling - the art of the tail

Let me tell you a story...

Back in my VMware days I managed a group of 4 Scrum teams. Lital Hassine was a team leader in the group I managed in VMware. At some point, Lital told me she has decided to leave VMware and start a new adventure. As always in these cases I used the opportunity and asked her to give me some feedback.

Asking for feedback from the people in my team is something that I'm doing routinely, not only does it allow me to understand how the world perceive me, it is one of the best tools for self-improvement; also, it allows the communication channel to be bi-directional and makes my life easier when I give the feedback to someone else.

But, still, getting feedback routinely is different from getting it before a person leave.

It makes it more dramatic to some extent. Since the feedback will echo forever. Echo forever. Forever. And ever....

No matter what you will do, unless you will engage with the person again in working relations, this feedback will stay in the air.

Now, Lital, since she is devoted to doing everything excellent, put a lot of thinking into my request and supplied great data for me to improve on.

One of her feedback points was:

"Gal, you should really tell more stories."

To tell you the truth, I didn't get it right away.

The time Lital had given me that feedback was around 2014, something like 2 years before storytelling as a concept for presentations or a leaders' tool was the most common buzzword in our industry.

At first, I didn't really understand what she meant, and more importantly why storytelling even matters.

I think that only a few years later during my days at Dropbox, I understood how important it is to tell engineers stories on the business.

All of us would like to be part of something bigger, to have a sense of belonging or a purpose.

And everyone loves a good story.

You need to tell stories to your developers in order for them to understand the business and to be connected to them - increasing their sense of belonging.

Steve Jobs once quoted: *"The most powerful person in the world is the storyteller. The storyteller sets the vision, values, and agenda of an entire generation that is to come"*.

Why? Because storytelling is the connecting-line between the company's mission, the organization's goals, the customers, and the makers that are doing the actual work.

It is also the thing which allows people to connect to the company's values.

Turns out, it is really hard to relate just to something that is written on a mail or as a poster on the wall.

If you are looking for a real, emotional connection, you need to do more than just **say** it. That is the reason that a lot of the time you see the company's values are accompanied by some images or sketches. Since it's much easier to connect to a visual or a drawing than just to the words themselves.

When you see a picture, you are building some mental image in your mind of the value the picture stands for, and this potentially can be burned in your head.

A story could have the same effect as an image - you are also starting to create some pictures of that story in your head; these are the things that you can emotionally connect to, that will be burned in your head.

Thus, if you have a goal about refocusing on your customer, you need to tell a story that will connect the employees to that...

There are several techniques for storytelling. I'm far from being an expert in this field, so I won't pretend to know how to teach you the storytelling theme. However, from my experience, you need to find your own storytelling style. For me, I find it easier if I'm the main character of the story.

Also, you need to practice. You need to practice telling stories since most of us are not storytellers by nature. I, for example, explicitly try to tell at least 1 story each month - It can be in a 1-on-1 meeting, in a presentation I'm doing in a conference, during my podcast, or in a group meeting. A lot of the time, while doing that, I feel awkward and even a bit embarrassed, but I'm getting there. One step at a time.

I've found that people that are able to tell a good story can, in most of the time, plot it in such a compelling way that a simple "improve our quality" need is turning into "delighting our customers" goal.

With some similarity, it is pretty boring or not aspiring to be part of a team that develops yet another cloud monitoring solution, but being part of a team that is helping that specific customer use your state of the art cloud monitoring solution, helping them to reduce the deforestation of the rainforests in Brazil.

Now, that is inspiring!

It's the same work, but not the same story.

It might seem just phrasing and paraphrasing. And to us engineers all this mambo jumbo crap usually seems like the nominal work part, or work about work. But we are not engineers now. We are engineering managers and part of our job is to explain why the engineering work matters. With a bit of rephrasing, suddenly the work your engineer is doing for creating a script to support tier 2 for fixing production issues on the customer's site feels to her as she just saved another tree.

You should always be careful from overdoing that, know your crowd and stay away from "over-awesomeness", since software engineers also have cynical sides in them.

The ideal in my view is to be super calm, relaxed, and nonchalant most of the time, and lift up the ethos and storytelling when needed - when there are challenging times, in high tide, when the kitchen is getting heated after a screaming customer, or when the blues is in the winds after a coworker is leaving the company (did you see what I did there).

MANAGEMENT EXERCISES

Exercise: Connect the company's mission to your team's tasks

1. Find out what is the mission of your company.

1.1 If that is not something that is written on all the walls, or is crystal clear, you should ask your manager. If they don't know, try asking the VP of Engineering.

1.2 If that doesn't help try asking someone from the product team.

1.3 If after all your inquiries the mission of the company is not cleared, at least the fact you've been poking around that would create a discussion - why don't we have a mission?!

2. Go over all the tasks that your team or your group is currently doing.

3. Try to map the tasks to the company's mission. It's not an easy thing to do. A lot of the time the mission is a bit vague, or abstract, or a one-sentence kind of a thing. Work through it. Try to find connected lines between the mission to the day-to-day stuff. Even if the line is dotted it's fine. Don't worry about it.

4. Now, you should have a written paper with a mapping of the tasks the team is doing to the mission. On each connected line between the task to a mission (or a sub-mission, if you could find such) write shortly

how the task connected to a mission. This step will supply extreme clarity for you.

5. You will probably find out that some tasks are left orphaned. Hmmm...Thinking time.

5.1. If you have a task that is not connected to the mission, ask yourself if it's really needed. Or maybe, just maybe, you can delete it, and have your team focus on other tasks instead.

5.2. If you decide that the task is a must-do, you should ask yourself, why is it not connected to the mission or to a sub-mission, maybe the mission itself needs refinement?

5.3. There are times where you need to work on tasks that are not part of the mission, or that connecting the line to it is a very complicated thing to do. It can be, for example, when you have a refactoring task, or when you need to do a lot of legacy investment. These tasks still might be with high priority. As a manager, you need to remember that these tasks need even more focus from you. The team probably feels a bit frustrated or confused - why are they working on stuff that are not connected to the mission. It is your job to explain to them the higher purpose, the motivation behind that, the story. Once it is clear to you, it should also be easy to explain.

6. Now, you have a map of lines between tasks to mission/sub-missions. You also have all the orphaned tasks and the stories behind them.

7. Spread the word! Tell the story! In one-on-one meetings, or in group gathering, or whenever - let the team know why the tasks they are working on is important. How it is connected to the mission, and if not, why are they working on it?

3 KEY TAKEAWAYS

- Knowledge workers need to have a purpose. It's critical for their ability to have a long-term drive.

- Purpose can and should be obtained by understanding the company mission and goals. And by knowing to connect the mission into the day to day tasks.

- You are a storyteller. It's an important skill. Learn it.

Chapter 6
Technology

THE SHOCKING TRUTH ABOUT HANDS-ON MANAGERS AND THE LIES YOU'VE BEEN TOLD ABOUT IT

THE *T* PART OF THE PUPPE*T*
PRINCIPLES FOR MANAGERS - 25 MINUTES READ

This chapter is going to upset many of you. If you are not up for it, consider skipping to the next one.

*J*ust the other day, one of my Tech Leads asked me whether they are expected to write code.

I've told the tech lead that this is the wrong question.

For context, in Dropbox, Google and a bunch of other technology companies there aren't any team leaders, there are Tech Leads (TLs) who manage the technical strategy and responsible on setting the right quality bar; and Engineering Managers (EMs) that are managing people's growth, the team's culture and the hiring process (obviously there are grey areas between TL role and an EM role, like which role is responsible for the project management aspects, but that is for a different story).

The "how much hands-on" question usually pops up once in a while, during a 1-on-1 meeting or on a weekly meeting with all the tech leads. A lot of the time the question arises after an employee satisfaction survey or during the yearly performance review - it is triggered after a discussion on the scope of impact.

It is, in fact, one of the most popular discussions in the software industry, right after spaces versus tabs and VIM versus PyCharm. "What is the hands-on percentage expected from a leader?"

The discussion on how much to invest in "hands-on" is legit.

It is clear that as a junior developer, you are doing 99% hands-on, which means most of the time you are coding.

However, for a more experienced engineer, let alone a tech lead or an engineering manager, it is unclear and unstructured how many percentages of your work should be hands-on coding versus other stuff.

It is not even super clear what "hands-on" means...does it mean coding? Does code review count? What about design review? Where do you stand on triaging a bug? Other?

This chapter is going to upset many of you, but the truth is that engineering manager that are 2nd line managers or above, should not be

hands-on (no matter how you define it). They can be. But they don't have to be, and it's definitely not their main job. Even first line managers that are seasoned enough and has a sizable team should not be hands on.

*The magnificent Lara Hogan, previously the VP of Engineering at Kickstarter and a coacher for managers said it sharply and bravely while answering to the following question: "**Do you think managing technical people is different from managing people from other backgrounds or with other skills?**"*

"Nope! I really don't. I know that this errs on the end of controversial, but really: humans are human. We share core needs like respect and clarity; we all benefit from managers who are transparent, trusting, and supportive.

I think that when you manage people in a particular discipline (like engineering), it helps to have an understanding of the kinds of problems that they solve, so you can develop a variety of ways to help them get 'unstuck.' This is true for any discipline! But the fundamentals of management skills are shared, I believe, across disciplines." This interview was published on the NY Times website by Nick Rockwell on 2018, Feb 23.

One of the funniest anomalies in our industry is the way companies create their management layers. In most companies, the best programmers are the ones that are "promoted" to be team leaders or engineering managers.

The problem is that often, though their programming capabilities are supreme, their management capabilities - with the emphasis on people management skills - are not.

Now, there is no doubt that for managing skilled, talented, eager (and a lot of the times vain) engineers you need to be smart enough and not to be a technophobe.

You also need to have a real passion for the hi-tech industry and for software development.

But you don't need to be the smartest person in the room, nor the best coder and even not the best technologist.

Not only that you do not need to be that person, but actually in most cases, you must not be that person. We will double click on that later.

Which technical skill do you need?

You need to have the ability to deep dive on system design.

You need to feel comfortable in discussions that are talking about complicated technical problems.

You need to have the ability to decide if creating a tech debt is reasonable and when is the time to pay that debt.

You need to have "a touch" or "a feeling" for asking the right questions.

You need to have the experience of knowing when to let go, when to push, and when to take risks.

You also need to have the ability to provide high-level guestimations or the courage to convince your CEO/VP/Director that giving an estimation is a waste of time.

You need to have the ability to hire smart developers for your team.

Wait...But if I'm not doing the "real" tech stuff, what should I be doing?

Well, hopefully, if you are at this point, you've read through the first parts of the PUPPET principles.

You should focus your time on people.

People, people, and then some more time on the people. In the rest of the time, you should focus on the culture of the organization and on the business.

Only then, if you absolutely must, go on and write some code. Do it for fun, for the soul, for feeling the beat. But not because it's your job. It is not.

HOW DOES THE AGILITY OF THE PUPPET PRINCIPLES COME INTO PLAY HERE?

When you are a first-time manager, it is quite clear that you should be very techie.

You understand technology and code, and one of your superpowers over your team, would be the fact you are always up to speed with the newest technologies, and you can give the team technical guidance on where to go, and how.

Often, in these stages, your charisma will be tech-oriented. People will follow you to the top of the hill since they trust your tech super-power.

As you have more people to manage and the scope and impact of the product you are in charge of increases, you'll have less time, and you'll drift away from the code.

As a Junior Manager, you should have very good **problem-solving** skills. A lot of your day-to-day work will be focused on helping your team's members remove impediments.

A small portion of the impediments won't be technical, like asks from another team, or requests to handle unrealistic requirements from the product management, but some would be purely technical; especially for the less experienced developers in the team - they are bound to encounter technical challenges they are not familiar with yet.

Here you'll have the chance both to help the team's execution, since you'll unblock it, but also to be a servant, and mentor your developer to be better.

When you are a **Senior Manager,** maybe you also have more people to manage, less time to do hands-on coding or code reviews...Other people in your group are doing that on a daily basis, so eventually by definition, they would be better than you at that. This is great. Don't fight it.

Other people in your group are more up to speed on the new tech innovations. That is wonderful!

What should you emphasize? You should foster a culture of technology, which would encourage learning and adopting new paradigms and tools. You should have an idea about what's new in the world (if you are not familiar at all with React JS or Angular JS and you still think JSP is the deal, it's a problem; but you don't need to understand the gory details of these frameworks) You should also be able to ask questions, on why we've incorporated the new mongo database.

But if you are the one that is suggesting to the team to move away from RabbitMQ and go with Apache Kafka instead....It's a signal that you might have a problem. You should not download the latest Cassandra database to your laptop and do a benchmark over it. You should read on the methodology that reduces waste and on how to build the perfect team.

You should ask yourself why the hell no one in my group brought up the option to use Cassandra before I did? Maybe they know I'll do it anyhow, so they don't feel there is room to grow there. Maybe they don't know how to do it, and they need some mentor to teach them (that is you, yes, this is your real job). Maybe the culture you fostered is not cultivating new tech (again - this is what you should focus on!).

There are managers that think they can do both of them. They are probably wrong.

Not all managers were born equal. Some are more tech-oriented than others. That's fine. The important thing is the priorities. At junior levels, you should go deep, understand the details and help your team be better at their technical capabilities. As you season you should focus on fostering the right tech culture and the environment for people to be a successful technologist.

THE PRACTICE - HOW TO NAVIGATE MANAGING PEOPLE IN A TECHNOLOGICAL WORLD?

TIP for a first-time manager: Avoid the temptation

Sometimes you might get tempted to take the more high-priority tasks or the ones that are more challenging from a technical perspective; this in most cases will fail. Either you will not succeed in meeting your commitment, or you will, but then your other management tasks will suffer.

For example, let's say that the team decided to move to a new cool database instead of the old, non-performing one. If you will do it, maybe - and that is a big maybe - this effort will be smoother, and the migration would be faster and with higher quality.

But you lost here two things, first of all, you lost the chance to mentor someone with less experience to gain the expertise, so that next time they can do that as good as you. The second thing is that in case this would be dragged since it is more complicated than expected, you will need to delay things that you should do with higher priorities, like 1-on-1 meetings with the people in the team, or hiring, or thinking on the next project.

You have a lot of balls juggling in the air. You should focus on the important ones first.

Furthermore, you need to let your team grow. If you keep doing the challenging stuff, your team will keep doing the small or uninteresting stuff. This is bad for motivation, bad for growth, and bad for the future of the company when you alone would not be able to cover all the challenging areas.

A better approach is to act as a wild card. From my experience, a lot of the top performing teams have a wild card in the team that provides enough flexibility to react for changes; one of the ways to achieve that is to have a developer in the team that is not pre-committed for high priority tasks. Then, this wild card is able to help people when they are blocked, or handle pebble surprised asks by the fields or product.

Note that as a junior team manager drifting too much away from the code is risky. Not because you need to be a world-class tech lead, but since it allows you to understand and relate better to the challenges your developers are facing in their day-to-day work; for example, **feel** in your hands the slowness of the development environment, the instability of remote debugging, or the boredom of the tasks the team is doing. Of course, you can get all of that from 1-on-1 meetings or team meetings, but feel it is better than hearing about it in this case.

Second, in this level, some (but not all) of your charisma would still be technical, and since you almost can't go wrong when leading by example, it would be good if your team sees you taking on yourself some technical challenges. It would be good if they will see your code skills during reviews, and your innovation while creating a cool script that monitors the number of flaky selenium tests and screens it on the big plasma screen.

Practical TIP: Don't feed them fish, teach them how to fish

The old Chinese proverb says: *"You give a poor man a fish and you feed him for a day. You **teach** him to fish, and you give him an occupation that will feed him for a lifetime"*.

Though this might seem trivial, I think that for juniors it is actually quite challenging.

It is so tempting to just find the bug, write the script, restore the IDE, write the SQL query or whatever. It's right in your comfort zone, it would be fast and would certainly unblock the team and push them to a faster execution.

Though it might seem like the right call tactically, it is the wrong call for the long run.

The right thing here would be to lead your developer to a different path from the one they took so far, by asking them questions, and by undermining (in the good sense of this term) their thinking.

Let's take a common example. Say your developer could not reproduce some UI bug opened by a customer. Since you have seen this before several times, you probably can reproduce the bug, find the root cause, and fix it in 9 minutes.

But maybe it would be better to ask your developer, how did he try to reproduce it? And then, ask him if he can think of other options to do it?

Now, this seems like a really stupid question, since you probably assume that if the answer to this question was yes, he should have done it already; but this is fake news. The truth of the matter is that just by asking junior developers if they can think of other approaches, their brain, in the attempt of not saying anything, will work hard to find answers.

Usually, the answers are lacking confidence which makes ton of sense, but you should keep on going. You should say: "well, yes Bob, maybe the production system acts a bit different from your development environment, so trying in production first seems like a great idea! You should try to remember that in the future as well since this sounds like a really good generic reproduction approach."

Then add: "Can you think of some other options to reproduce it if that won't work?"

Why? It's important to have junior developers get used to thinking that there are almost always several approaches for finding the root cause of a problem and several options for creating a solution.

Now, the problem they are facing is not that they cannot reproduce - The problem is what to try first?

After the developer had succeeded to reproduce the bug, not only did they gain the experience of solving this specific bug, also they have practiced the skills of thinking more broadly on a problem, and maybe most importantly, their confidence was built, since eventually they reproduced and solved the problem, and not you.

By the way, in the example above, I assumed that you know the answer since you've seen it before. But, even if you haven't seen this before, and you are not quite sure how to reproduce it, and you feel that you must take the steering wheel and let your hands fly on the keyboard in order to start analyzing it. Don't. Just don't. Try to put words in your mouth and think about what is it that you'd try. Try to ask the developer some questions that would lead them to the same conclusion. And if you still can't, it's time to do some pair programming with them. Let them drive the wheel while you are sitting by their side and helping them navigate.

If you are a director in a BIG company or a VP of R&D of a large startup you still have a lot of problem-solving to do, but they tend to be less technical per se and more oriented into people, product, and project management, but we'll get to that down the road.

TIP for the director: keep calm and ask questions

The other important skill in this technical domain is the ability to make **good (and fast) decisions**. This will be important at any level of management.

At first, as a junior team lead, you will have to take a major part in the decision of which technology to choose or on what is the best design pattern for this case, but also later on your teams will come to you when they face major technical junctions.

At this point, you will need to be able to make high-level technical decisions without knowing all the details and without "feeling" the code. Also, what some of you will lose at this point - and it's perfectly legit - is the tech advantage you used to have. You might have heard of some new cool ultra-scaled database or distributed queue technology, but you hadn't had the time to download the latest version of this queue and to try it yourself, for doing a small benchmark proof of concept with other queues.

The ideal play would be to delegate 99% of the technical decisions to the people that are actually doing the technical work. This is the right play for a lot of reasons (empowerment, less bureaucracy, and more), but still, there would be times - depending on your teams' structure, compositions, and talent - you'll have to make some high-level technical decisions.

As a director you have a lot of experience; you were an engineer once, a team leader, a group manager, and now you are a Director or the VP of Engineering. You've been around. Even if you sometimes don't *feel* it or if you suffer from the Impostor syndrome, you should have good intuition on what's right and wrong. All you need to do now is to ask questions, a lot of them.

There are several basic techniques you can use and practice if you don't feel that asking technical questions are your second nature.

I'll share here two of these techniques.

The 5 Whys technique - *"**5 Whys** is an iterative interrogative technique used to explore the cause-and-effect relationships underlying a particular problem.[1] The primary goal of the technique is to determine the root cause of a* bug *or problem by repeating the question "Why?" Each answer forms the basis of the next question. The "5" in the name derives from an anecdotal observation on the number of iterations needed to resolve the problem."* Taken from Wikipedia.

Like a lot of the good things in software development practices, this technique has originated from the East and specifically from the Toyota System. This is a magical system of rules, processes, and techniques which create the way Toyota manufactures cars.

Let's take an example for how to use the five whys.

Say your team is developing a product running in the cloud as SAAS (SAAS is an acronym for software as a service; in this context, it means, that the bug in production impact most of your customers). Now, there is a report on a bug in production, where users were constantly getting kicked out. After the bug was fixed, you probably want to make sure that similar bugs will not happen again, or that if they do happen, they would be detected quicker, and fixed faster.

In order to do that, you need to understand the root cause, but you are not familiar with the code itself. You need to start asking questions.

1) Why were the customers kicked out?

Because there was a timeout that was introduced for testing purposes that got into production.

2) Why was it introduced to production?

Because someone deleted the code that gated it by mistake.

3) Why was the code deleted by mistake?

Because you've made us work 14 hours a day and after the 11th hour we've started inserting stupid bugs.

4) Why the stupid bugs were not caught by code review?

Because we are not reviewing code that was supposed to be covered by tests.

5) Why didn't the tests catch the bug?

Because the build was failing anyhow (for other test suites) and the developer was in a hurry to push this to production, so he marked skipped-the-queue (commit without running tests).

By asking 5 whys, the team would need to dive deep enough in order to give satisfying answers.

An anti-pattern to watch out for is falling into the court scene. Make sure it is clear you are not blaming anyone, nor do you look for the culprit. The state of mind you need to explicitly declare is that you only care about the future - how are we getting better, and not what have we done wrong.

If it feels tricky, you can try replacing the why with a "what can we do in the future?"

The second technique you can use is **templates.**

There are a lot of common questions for common technical scenarios. You can create for yourself a template for each of the common use cases.

Let's take an example of a nice template that can be applied when a team presents the post-mortem for a SEV (in Dropbox, SEV is the name of a serious bug in production impacting customers). Without going into all the detail, the template consists of questions on the SEV's lifecycle:

Is the team happy with the length of time it took them to discover the problem? And why?

Is the team happy with the way they communicate to the rest of the world on the SEVs existence?

The examples above are bugs related since bugs are common and are easy to give as an example even if one does not have the relevant context or domain knowledge. Still, with a bit of modifications, they can also be applied to broader, high-level design decisions.

TIP for the director: delegate and let them fail

If you feel that your team keeps coming to you with requests to make a decision on purely technical aspects, you might have a problem.

From my experience, it may be folded to one of the following:

Your team is not experienced or talented enough to make technical decisions - you need to fix it ASAP (see ahead).

Or, your team does not feel empowered to make decisions. They are afraid of failing.

I remember that a few years ago, I met in a conference a VP engineering working for a successful American corporate - He explained in details how they are working really hard to make sure that the engineering culture empowers all the decisions to be made by the team and not by anyone else.

This is so simple and so true; the team has more knowledge and details than their managers, so they should feel empowered to make decisions. This is also one of the core essences of implementing agile using Scrum. The team is the center - they have the knowledge, skills, and empowerment to move autonomously.

If lack of autonomy and empowerment is not the problem, then maybe your team is afraid of failing.

You need to create a culture in which failing is cool, it is acceptable - moreover it is expected.

The only thing that matters is to learn from the failures. If we are going back to the bug in production, for example then the state of mind the team should have is: okay, it was a failure, what can we learn from that? How can we get better?

The best phrasing for that is a culture of claim without blame. Have people claim their failure and take accountability to learn from that, but no blaming whatsoever. Easier said than done.

TIP: Learn from best practices

We don't know it all and we shouldn't.

But we should have enough context and network to be familiar with similar companies that have solved problems we are tackling right now. One of the things a manager should know how to do is to learn by reading or by meeting relevant people.

Imagine that you had someone else in your company that has experience in a similar technical challenge, like how to move from relational database to a NoSQL one. You would have consulted with her for sure; you would have your team go ahead and ask her experience, for tips, for potential problems.

But, even if you don't have that kind of experience in your company, if you are a senior leader, you've been around. You have built a network and you should use it; try to find a relevant company that has the experience and is willing to share, and then create the connections with your team.

Besides gaining the experience, you will also gain the exposure of your team to the community which is always an opportunity to grow.

4 TIPs for the seasoned leader: The "curse of knowledge"

The curse of knowledge is a cognitive bias that was first illustrated By Elizabeth Newton in 1990. Newton, a Stanford University graduate student in psychology, did a simple research in which she assigned people to one of two roles: "tapper" or "listener". The tappers had to tap some well-known song and the listeners had to guess it. Though 50% of the tappers predicted that the listeners would guess right, the real results were that only 2.5% were right.

We see it all the time in real life as well. Leaders that have already implemented some process or have a great intuition on setting a goal and they assume their team has the same experience, and knowledge; thus, would easily follow their guidance. We are wrong.

Lately me and my colleagues wanted to adjust some of the engineering processes in the organization to be a bit more agile. We have all worked in Scrum, Kanban or other agile methodologies years ago. We've seen it succeeding, and we've seen it fail. We've seen the basics, and we've seen advanced and more customized methods of agile implementations. We were under the impression the entire team has experienced agile before, in some way or another, and has the same scars and the same learnings.

We were shocked when the questions we got from the team were much more basic than we thought we would get. It was about the core principles of agile and not on the stuff we'd had in mind to fine tune.

We see this all the time, not only in engineering organizations, but all around. The most obvious demonstration of that is in the academy, where you take a seasoned professor, and put them in front of 1st year students.

When I was learning bioinformatics, in the computer science department; in multiple occasions during Calculus course, Professor P explained something, over and over again, and it was always along the same pattern

Prof: this is really very basic

Us:

Prof:

us:

prof:

Going back to the leadership and management world. What are some best practices to handle this "curse of knowledge" cognitive bias?

1. Stop making assumptions. Trust, but also verify. Ask - what did the team understand? follow up.

2. Always, always and always start with the why. Even if it's obvious, the why is the ground floor of alignment. You can't start to build the house from the roof.

3. Don't forget your mentor hat. You are not just a manager, or an executor. You are a leader, you are here to grow others, teach and mentor - do it.

4. There isn't such a thing as over communication.   Communicate. Communicate. Then, communicate some more.

Exercise: Create your first template for technical questions

In this exercise you will create your first template for how to ask technical questions that would allow you to dive into technical decisions making.

The template is agile by nature and should evolve over time.

1. Think about the last time you had to do a deep dive into a technological decision. Maybe it was a post-mortem on a production failure, perhaps it was a decision on specific technology, maybe it was a question on threat modeling or handling high-level scale issues.

2. Write the topic down. Reflect on it a bit.

3. Now, write at least five questions you could have asked the team in order to get some data points. Try using WH open questions and not a different kind.

4. Now, pick another technical discussion from the last couple of months.

5. Write it down.

6. Check which of the same five questions above, with some minor changes, could have applied in that case as well

Result: The common questions, might be the base of your template in the future. It's an agile list of questions. You should adjust it as you go.

3 KEY TAKEAWAYS

- Engineering Manager is a profession. It's not a promotion from a developer role, and it's not a step in the way.

- Technological "hands-on" is not a critical thing for a people manger. In most cases, it would even get in the way.

- You need to build for yourself frameworks that would allow you to make technical decisions without doing hands-on work.

Chapter 7
A methodological break

BELIEVE IN WHAT YOU DO!

2 MINUTES READ

"To have long-term success as a coach or in any position of leadership, you have to be obsessed in some way." This was quoted by Pat Riley, one of the most important NBA basketball coaches.

If you see your profession as a manager, as a coach, be obsessed about it. For me, a manager is not a promotion from doing hands-on work. It is not a step in the way. It's definitely not a solution for being bored or out of growth options.

For me, an **engineering manager is a profession**.

It is a tedious one. You don't get immediate satisfaction anymore.

As a manager it is hard to make changes, but you must keep trying. Your work is to make the team better.

Remember that words are your art. Mails, chat applications, and meetings are your sword and shield.

Don't be bothered by the fact that you spend most of the time reading and writing mails. Don't feel ashamed that your entire day was back-to-back meetings.

This is your job. This is what you do.

Your road to take is the one that makes People and team better; Even if it seems a bit tedious at times, we need to put very high expectations, and to coach the team how to get there.

You need to be opinionated about the cUlture you want to have in your teams and to work our way through it. We need to reiterate over and over about our Processes to make sure they are needed and crisp and to see if we can transform them into culture instead.

You should work to understand the Product and the market. You should get to know the customer that you are creating a product for. Get to know the mission and the goals. Understand how the businEss operates. Once you do, you will be able to tell the story of purpose to the team.

Don't feel embarrassed that you spend less time and energy on being Technology hands-on. It's not the most important thing.

You should spend your time and energy on hiring the right people, coaching them to fulfill their talent, focus them to work on the right things, and mentor them to do it in the right way. This is the basics. It's not enough, but it's enough to start with. What else?

The next 2 chapters are a glimpse of management tips and practices that are beyond the PUPPET principles. In my mind they are 2 of the most important tools a manager needs to practice.

Chapter 8
The 1:1 meeting

THE SINGLE MOST IMPORTANT TOOL
IN A MANAGER TOOLBOX

13 MINUTES READ

A few years back, I was pushed into a position where I had 20 people in my team reporting directly to me. It is an unhealthy situation, and I do not recommend you follow that pattern.

It was a temporary state that lasted for a few months.

At some point, during a sugar break with one of my colleagues, a fellow engineering manager, they were surprised to find out that I still hold weekly one-on-one meetings with all the people that report to me.

They asked me how I manage my time with 20 meetings a week just on one-on-ones? And more importantly, why do I do it?

They even added a short calculation where correctly argued that doing one-on-one meetings with 20 people means that something like 2 days of the week is being consumed only for that. That does not leave a lot of time to do other stuff.

Their math was correct.

THE 1:1 MEETING IS THE MOST IMPORTANT TOOL IN YOUR MANAGER'S TOOLBOX.

During the years, I've heard all kinds of managers claiming that it is required only if you are working in large companies, and you don't know what your team is working on. This is bullshit.

In this chapter you'll see why 1:1 meeting is so important, and how to conduct it effectively.

WHAT NOT TO DO IN ONE-ON-ONE MEETINGS?

I'm starting with what not to do in a one-on-one meeting, since this is a very common misunderstanding of the one-on-one tool. Abusing this tool can actually have a negative impact.

One-on-one meetings are **not a project's status report**. You should not spend 30 minutes with a developer understanding what they did last week, or what is their plan for the next. This is not what the meeting is all about. There are other more efficient ways to get that information. There are other meetings for that, other processes and other tools to help you stay up to date on the project's statuses. One-on-one is not one of them.

You can certainly use the project, and the challenges they are facing in order to direct the conversation to the right places, but this is not the main thing. It's an amuse-bouche for the main course, but it's not the lunch itself.

5 REASONS WHY TO HOLD ONE ON ONE MEETINGS REGULARLY

We have figured out what not to do in one-on-one meetings, but why are they so important? There are several reasons for that, and I'm going to elaborate on the top five reasons to hold them regularly:

1. The one-on-one meeting at first and foremost should be a **safe zone** - a place where the engineer can feel they bring any agenda and discuss it freely. It can be either something personal they want to share, like a change in their family status, health or other personal related things that they feel like sharing. **This is your place to show care.** They might share it since they feel it impact or can impact their work, or just since they trust you and you've created a safe zone for them to offload. They can also use this safe place to share their feelings on the team or team members - Are they happy with the team? Do they feel included? Any big conflicts with team members they would like your input and so on?

2. The 2nd thing you should use the one-on-one meeting for is in order to help people **grow**. When I say 'grow' in this context, I

mean it in the most generalized way out there. Helping the developer grow by giving them feedback and recognition and by talking with them on their career aspirations; helping them navigate it. I've already mentioned a lot of times in this book, that the most important thing in management is the people and supporting their development. The one-on-one tool is probably the best tool in your toolset for doing that. It's a time that is dedicated - both by the engineer and yourself - for that goal. As explained, you are not talking about work, or the task's status. Now, when the expectations were set, it's pretty straightforward to move to a state of mind of talking about feedback, career, and self-development.

3. The other side of the growth and feedback aspects of the one-on-one meetings is the **bi-directional feedback**. The meeting should be a place where the engineers can and should feel empowered to bring up feedback on you, on the organization, on the process, and on the culture. You should not expect to get that on each and every one-on-one meeting, but you should make sure you set up the scenery in order to empower it. You should talk about **continuous improvement**. And how it is important for

the organization to get better. You should talk about your expectations from engineers, to carry on their critiquing glasses, since it means they are aiming higher. Not just for themselves, but from the company as well. This is important not just for getting the "what can be better" input, but also since it would make the feedback street bi-directional. And that would help the feedback (both ways) to not fall on deaf ears.

4. **Purpose** and motivation are the 4th reason to hold one-on-one meetings. We've already mentioned the importance of purpose and connecting the business goals to the day-to-day tasks of an individual. Purpose is the fuel for running long distances. Since company's high-level goals can sometimes feel distant and amorphic, managers should work hard in connecting them to the day-to-day explicitly as they can. This is one of the ways to make sure the people in the team feel motivated.

5. Lastly, a one on one meeting is an opportunity for the manager to push their agendas. Occasionally, as managers, you are **leading a change**. A change in the processes the team is doing, or in the culture, or maybe in the project the team owns. At times, since change is a tricky thing

to manage, you'd like to bring people to an agreement or an alignment as individuals before you are doing that with the entire group. It may help to reduce tension, provide a place where concerns and ideas, can be heard with less judgement and more. This is true not just for a manager-reportee relationship.

There are (at least) five reasons for managers to hold one-on-one meetings regularly: provide a safe zone, feedback and growth, continuous improvement, purpose and motivation, and to push your agenda.

There are probably other good reasons as well, and there are also reasons for the individual contributor to hold such meetings - such, managing your career path, managing up, and more - but this is a topic for a different book.

SETTING THE SCENERY

FREQUENCY OF THE ONE ON ONE MEETINGS

One-on-one meetings with direct reports need to happen once a week. Less than that would create a big gap between the meetings, and specifically for reason number one of creating the safe zone, this is not acceptable.

Even if you declare and hold "open door" policy (or you are seating in the open space and have no doors to open), some people would not feel comfortable approaching you with off topics, in an informal manner. For that reason alone, it's required to hold the meeting weekly.

HOW LONG SHOULD THE MEETING BE?

The minimum time for one-on-one meeting should be 30 minutes.

It is totally fine if now and then some of the meetings would be much shorter, but you should still save a slot in the calendar for 30 minutes at least.

Should you hold longer one-on-one meetings? Depends.

First of all, it depends on the number of people you manage directly. If you manage 20 people directly, doing 1-hour one-on-one meetings would leave 2 days a week to other stuff. That is not enough.

Second, it depends on the reportee, if they are new to the organization, they might need more time with you than others. If they are tech leaders or people managers, you might want to hold a 1-hour meeting with them, since you also need to talk on their reportees (your indirect reports).

WHERE AND WHERE NOT TO HOLD THE ONE ON MEETINGS?

Basically, it is advisable to hold the meeting in a room.

A room with visible walls/door. While this might feel obvious to some, it is not. one-on-one meetings should not be held in the open space, nor in the team's room, nor in the cafeteria. They should be in a room, where the only people in the room are the manager and the team members.

You should break this rule if you need to break the routine. More on that in a few more lines.

THE ONE-ON-ONE MEETING STRUCTURE AND CONTENT

The content of the one-on-one meeting is derived from the 5 reasons I've mentioned above to hold that meeting from the first place - provide a safe zone, feedback and growth, continuous improvement, purpose and motivation, and to push your agenda.

Don't worry about going through all of the five points. This is not going to happen. But alternately, you should touch them.

You should start most of the one-on-one meetings with a casual friendly 'What's up? How's life? How was the weekend? How is it to come back from a long vacation? You were sick last week, are you better now? How is the new apartment?'

You can replace it with talking about your weekend, vacation, coming out of a cold if you feel this would create a more bi-directional conversation.

Now, you need to move on to the rest of the topics you had in mind.

It's a matter of style really, but at that point, I'm heading in one of two ways. Either I'm asking something like: "What are we talking about today"? This signals the person that they are responsible for the agenda. It opens the door for a trust place talk, but not just.

Another approach I'm using is that, I say nothing. I just keep quiet. I'm shutting up. There is a psychological effect where 2 people are sitting in a room together, they cannot stay silent. One of them is going to break it. If it ain't going to be you, it is going to be them. See more about how managers should really learn to shut up in a short post I published entitled, "_Are You a Manager? Shut Up_!" in Medium 2018, November.

After the person has come up with at least one topic they wanted to discuss it is time to move to my agenda - feedback, recognition, career growth, motivation, or anything I have prepared in advanced.

This is a critical note. especially if you are a new manager, **you need to prepare for your one-on-one meetings**. You should make sure that during the week, you gather input and topics for discussions, and before the meeting, you have a clear agenda of what you want to talk about.

ONE-ON-ONE FOLLOW UP

Many times, issues that came up in the 1:1 require a follow up. Either by yourself or the team. Make sure to follow up. This will reinforce your credibility and demonstrate the importance you give to these meetings. As an example, if your reportee was wondering about a potential LOA (Leave of Absence) make sure you go back to them with the company's policy before they reach out to you and to remind you on their request.

WHY YOU SHOULD NEVER CANCEL A 1:1 MEETING

A while back, after a developer in my team decided to leave the company, as usual I've asked for feedback. They told me all kinds of things that were good and less, but the thing that stuck was the fact they were saying, that I've always cancelled our 1:1 meeting. The fact was that I have never ever cancelled a 1:1 meeting with them, and de facto I've spent more time with them than with anyone else in the team

I did however, occasionally, move the meetings from the original time, to a few hours later or even a full day delay. If I'd only known then what I know now, what you know now. I would have never postponed it, or at least been a lot more sensitive to communicate that the right way.

HOW TO BREAK THE ROUTINE

In some cases, you'll see that your 1:1 meetings are boring. Quiet. People are not bringing enough data points to talk on, and you don't have enough to share as well.

In these cases, I'm advising you to move out of the meeting room. Go for a walk, go for a coffee outside, go to lunch together. Anything that is not regular. Just make sure you keep the first rule above and are not doing that in the open space in front of other people.

There are other ideas that can help you break the routine, like preparing a bunch of generic questions on cards, that might be relevant to such meetings, and allowing the engineer to randomly choose one card, and start from there...

SOME MORE ADVANCED TOPICS

There are a lot more to one on one meetings:

How to handle 1:1 on video chats, while you are working remotely/distributed?

How to manage 1:1 meetings with introverts?

How to understand from the meetings the pulse of the team?

1:1 with indirect report - How frequent? How not to overstep your leads?

Since a man has to eat, we will keep something for the next book.

16 MINUTES READ

A few years back, in one of the companies I've used to work in, we discussed the option to transfer mandate from a team that is located in the headquarters offices in the Silicon Valley, to my team that was located in Tel Aviv.

The idea was unifying several domains that had a lot in common from product perspective; and therefore, give my team more ownership, empowerment, and the ability to execute on large scope projects with minimal integration needed.

There were several topics to discuss before making such a decision to move ownership from one team to another:

- Does my team have the muscle to handle such work? Until that time, my team was doing end-to-end features, but had less knowledge around infrastructure development.

- Headcount issues   do we have enough people to take this new domain or do we need to hire new ones? How much training is required?

- We had to think about what the team that is located in the headquarters would do after they are dissolved.

- And more and more...

*It took us **9 months** to make the decision, and only after a full year did, we actually executed upon it.*

During that period of 9 months, five to seven very senior engineering managers and product managers met weekly over video conference calls.

There were 8 documents which were created over that process. One of them listed the possible risks and mitigations, one was about the timelines, another one described the staffing and headcount asks, one was about future roadmap, and so on and so forth.

During these 9 months, we didn't gain new information that we didn't possess in the beginning.

We've clarified some things, brainstormed, argued, agreed, and disagreed, over and over again, but there was no new input that we didn't have at point 0.

Eventually, we made the decision to do the transfer. A few months later, we came to the conclusion that the transfer was a bad decision and we've reverted it.

During that period of 9 months a lot has changed.

The company has shifted gears, some people left, others have joined, the market was not the same. So much had happened that the decision we needed to take in point 0 was almost not relevant to the one we had to take after 9 months.

If it wasn't clear, I'll explicitly say it - it took us 9 months to make the decision, since we were scared. **We were fearful of making the wrong decision, so we didn't make any decision at all.**

One of the most basic foundations of a good manager is the ability to make decisions.

Making decisions effectively is hard.

In the last few years a lot of the leading companies are driving a very data-driven decision-making process. It means that they are gathering a lot of data, analyzing it in a logical way, and trying to make decisions based on it.

Some companies are using a lot of experiments in order to validate their thinking. This is usually done for product-related decisions, for example, what would create more user's traction, a round button or a square one?

It means that they are performing some scoped trial in order to get a better feel or to have more input before they move forward to make the decision. These kinds of product experiments are statistics based and named A/B testing as you are comparing two versions of a single variant.

When it comes to none-product decisions, I think it is very hard to really measure the quality of decisions in our line of work.

It is pretty easy to **feel** if the decisions are taken fast or slow, but surprisingly this is not the main problem. **The real problem of slow or no decision-making culture is the atmosphere created as a byproduct.**

In organizations that decisions making is slow, delayed, or just not taken, the entire culture is slow and delayed.

If you are not driven by making a decision, if you are not biased to action, then when you conduct a meeting, the meeting by nature will be useless. It would not have an end-goal. It will be a long chattering not converging into making a decision.

It will make the people disengaged. They will feel apathy since they know that whatever they do, it won't impact anything, because there are no decisions taking place.

A lot of the times when managers and leaders are not making decisions fast enough (or at all), it's contagious. You take examples from your leaders.

Soon, individual contributors will not make decisions as well. At that point, the organization would be practically paralyzed.

The bottom line is that as a manager you need to train yourself in making fast decisions. And reiterate on them.

THE PRACTICE - HOW TO FEARLESSLY MAKE DECISIONS FAST.

The theory and practice of decision-making is taught over several courses in the university, but in this section, I'd like to synthesize several basic tips that would help you make decisions specifically as engineering manager in the software industry.

TIP: Make explicit bets

In the excellent book "Thinking in Bets" by the Psychologist and poker player, Annie Duke, she is saying that de facto making decisions is a bet, and you cannot guarantee its result. Moreover, sometimes great decisions lead to poor results, and poor decisions can lead to great results.

In addition, in real life, just like in Poker and unlike Chess, we don't have the entire data upfront when we need to make a decision. Not only that, but sometimes the decisions output might not be completely in our hands. There might be dependencies, more outside factors and so on.

But if that is the case, what you need to do is to be explicit at the fact that you are making a bet, be ready with a backup plan if the decision turned out to be the wrong bet, and reduce as much as possible the energy consumption of trying to come up with the "right decision".

If you will think in bets, not only would the quality of the decisions should be improved, but also the time and energy you put in the decision-making process would be minimized.

This is a key point. A lot of the time, it seems to us that the main problem with slow or no decision-making is the time that had been spent on the decision process or the time that we lost since we didn't get any decision. But **the real issue is the energy that is being drained**.

For example, if we are looking on the above example of the ownership transfer, it's not just the fact that we have spent 1 hour, multiplied by 5 executives multiplied by 36 weeks for a total of 180 hours. This equals a full-time of one software engineer for an entire month!

It is not even the fact that we lost 9 months that we could have made better progress as a company.

It is mostly about the fact that the parties involved got drained of energy. Which caused their day-to-day motivation to drop and for them to lose their flow and to work in a non-optimal way. It is about the destruction effect this decision dragging had on the organization's culture. Slow or no decision-making atmosphere is contagious.

What should you do? **Avoid paralysis analysis at all cost. Take bets. Smart and measurable bets.**

For example, a few months later, while the 9-moths episode was still burning my bones, we had to make another decision. There was a new product area we thought on tackling. There were 3 options on the table: decide not to tackle it, tackle it, or delay the decision until we will have more data.

There were several risk factors in tackling the area now without getting more data points. We didn't have a product manager that was an expert in this field, we weren't sure if the company's leadership would support it, and before diving into the technical architecture of the solution it was hard to estimate the complexity of work and the number of dependencies to other parts of the organization.

After one-hour brainstorming, we decided to take the risk (the bet) and put 4 people in that area for a month. During that month, we tried to understand the complexity and dependencies and also to create a PoC (Proof of Concept) so we can demo to the company leadership. According to our guestimation, there was around a 30% chance that after one month we will get a "no go".

You need to understand that this is not a trivial decision to make. 30% risk is a lot. It means that if we eventually decide on a "no go" we've just spent 4 months (1-month times 4 developers) that we could have spent elsewhere.

We took a bet. We did it, after understanding the risk (30%) and its impact (4 months lost), and while doing this with our eyes open (we let the team know that we are in a validation phase and we are taking a risk). We had a backup plan, or at least a contingency plan (we knew that after 1 month, if we were not getting the green light, we were halting this effort).

An important disclaimer to make here, is that there are some areas in the work you should do your best to avoid risks as much as possible and to minimize the betting effect. An example of that is hiring. Since by nature hiring is a risk-full event which has a potential for huge negative impact, you should do what you can to minimize the betting factor.

A similar approach to Annie Duke's betting mechanism is coming from a different world all together. It is called the perfection of imperfection.

THE PERFECTION OF IMPERFECTION

Photo by Holger Link on Unsplash

In traditional Japanese, **Wabi-sabi** (侘寂) is a world view centered on the acceptance of transience and imperfection. It's the understanding that beauty can be found in something that is imperfect, impermanent, and incomplete.

This is one of the most crucial things on making decisions in a timely manner.

You need to understand that the surroundings of getting the non-trivial decisions would almost never be perfect.

It is almost an axíōma; and the proof is that if it was perfect, meaning we have all the data, there are no unknowns, the trade-offs are clear, then making the decision would be trivial; but we are focusing on the interesting decisions, not on the trivial ones.

Q.E.D.

The idea is that you need to let go. This is crucial for a manager, not just upon making decisions on a rocky ground, but also when delegating work to subordinates.

You need to accept the beauty of making decisions on incomplete data.

The bottom line is that you need to make fast decisions, validate the results, and if they need to be adjusted go on and adjust once you have new data.

TIP: Delegate, empower, and trust

One of the tech leads in my team encountered some weird behavior while monitoring a new feature in production; the tech lead sent me a direct message (DM) in Slack describing the findings.

"Would you like to open a SEV for that"? The leader kept asking. We were sitting in a large open area and I could practically hear his mechanic keyboard getting pounded.

(SEV is a terminology describing a serious bug happening right now in production impacting customers).

"What do you think, should we?" I've asked back shortly.

"If my suspicion turns out to be true, it might be a serious matter." He mumbled.

This doesn't really qualify as an answer, I'd thought to myself. Since I asked whether we should file a SEV, not if this has the potential for being a serious matter.

"Hmmm...that sounds true, but do you think we should open a SEV"? I kept my position.

<Keyboard typing for a while now>.

"I don't know". The short answer after a lot of typing suggests that a lot of deletion and thinking have been made here. I could see the tech lead is in distress.

"What information or data do you need in order to make the decision?" This was my cue to hand-off the fishing rod.

Since the tech lead had the answer all along, it was just a matter of pulling the right strings in order to make him think.

"Well, assuming we know the probability of that to be a real issue is high, and the impact is serious, the only question is if we have someone that is doing less critical things to handle it, right? Actually, I think that this is the most critical thing right now, and we should shift at least one person to look at.Yeah, let's open a SEV".

Bingo!

As a manager it is often the case that people in the team would ask you to make a decision. If possible, you should throw the ball back at them, empowering them to make the decision on their own.

You should take under account they might make the wrong decision. That's fine. Don't worry about that.

Trust them. Let them fail and use their failures as learning opportunities.

Note that there are some cases (not a lot), where the team cannot make a decision. This can happen since they don't have a wider context, or it involves other teams.

If you frequently find out that the team does not have enough context, it might be an indication you have a problem. Maybe they do not feel enough empowerment, or there is too much hierarchy in the organization, or just not enough communication. Either way you need to find the underlying cause and fix it.

TIP for the audacious and seasoned leader: use 2nd order thinking if you'd like to be exceptional

Let's play a game.

Imagine that you are in an all-hands gathering of your company. For the sake of this story, assume that there are 140 people in the room. Some of them are software developers, some of them are product owners, others are user experience (UX) designers, and maybe a handful of managers as well.

Now, each person in the room needs to choose a number between 0 and 100, inclusive. And we can assume the numbers are restricted to real numbers only.

The winner of the game is the one that their chosen number is the closest to the 2/3 average of all the numbers that were chosen in the room.

Now, take a minute and choose that number.

Maybe your line of thought was as follows: I don't know what the people in the room will choose, so let's assume they each chose a random number between 0 to 100. Assuming a normal distribution, which makes sense, if we have no other data, the average would be around 50. 2/3 of 50 is around 33. Since your goal is to be close to 33 as much as possible, you choose 33.

But, wait, if you have followed that simple logic, maybe it is worthwhile to assume that the other people in the room will follow a similar logic as well. Since you are all working in the same company, and are sharing a similar profession, it is kind of safe to assume that you share some basic logic commonalities.

If the other people in the room choose 33 as well, the average won't be 50. It would be 33.

2/3 of 33 is 22.

Maybe you would be better to choose 22.

But wait, if you choose 22, maybe other people in the room would follow that same logic and will also choose 22...

A few more iterations like that and you'll soon see that the "right number" to choose is 0.

But wait, are you really sure that all the people in the room will follow your exact same logic? Maybe some of them won't think the same way, maybe some of them were occupied in their phone, and didn't pay attention to all the details?

Maybe some of them have a lucky number, and they always choose it and are not following any social or math logic.

The point of this game is not to see if you choose 0 or 17 or 42. It is a known equilibrium in game theory and you can read more about the *Pareto Efficiency*.

The point of this game was to demonstrate different levels of thinking.

In his exceptional book, The Most Important Thing, **Howard Marks,** hits on the concept of **second-order thinking**, which he also refers to as second-level thinking.

While *"First-level thinking is simplistic and superficial, and just about anyone can do it..."*, the 2nd level thinkers take into account a lot of things like, The range of possible outcomes; what's the probability I'm right; what are the follow-ups; How could I be wrong?

According to Marks' book: *"First-level thinkers think the same way as other first-level thinkers do about the same things, and they generally reach the same conclusions. By definition, this can't be the route to superior results."*

Obviously, it's hard to come up with a real example to 2nd level thinking but recall the tip we had on the impact of organization structure change that potentially can impact the company's culture. A first level thinking might just consider the organization structure itself. Does it make sense, from people roles and responsibilities, to the projects scope and required outlook. A second level thinking would be to think what the impact to the company's culture would be, or what would happen if some of our assumptions on the current structure will break. For example, a key person would leave the company just after the reorg. Would the new structure be flexible enough to handle it?

Since most people are doing first-level thinking, if you want to be exceptional, you need to invest time in 2nd level thinking. Obviously, it would also introduce a risk of being wrong and byproduct to get results that are less than average. But it's a risk you need to take if you want to be great.

While it's probably not true for all, for me another advantage of 2nd-level thinking is that it is just more fun to swim against the current.

You need to remember though, that first level of thinking, which is the more intuitive one, and by nature the most direct and simple one, can sometimes be superior to any 2nd, 3rd or nth level. In some cases, simplicity is just about right. KISS - Keep It Simple Stupid - was already mentioned in this book several time.

So, what should you do? Should you kiss or should you deep? As I said in the very beginning of this book, this book is not a recipe or a script that will take you hand-in-hand to the promised land; I don't believe such a book exists. This book will make you think. You and only you can develop your management style...

Exercise: Make a decision

1. Look back at the previous 3 weeks.

2. Come up with 1 decision that is still waiting on your table. It can be a big thing like the new work-stream you need to establish, or a small thing like a possible tweak to the code review process.

3. Understand why you didn't make a decision so far. Were you lacking data? Do you fear from the result?

4. Try to come up with 2 possible outcomes for the decision. Calculate the risk of making one decision over another.

5. Make the decision. Doesn't that feel good?

6. Try to come up with second level thinking to this. Can you think about that differently? What will happen if the decision you've made will lead to partial results, how will that play out?

7. Don't forget to monitor the result.

3 KEY TAKEAWAYS

- The real problem of slow decision-making culture is the atmosphere created by it.

- Don't be afraid of imperfection. Accept it. Know the risk. Iterate on the results, to make the decision.

- Diversify your decision-making techniques.

Chapter 10
Summary - beyond the PUPPET principles

HAS THE JOURNEY ENDED? IT HAS JUST BEGUN

1 MINUTE READ

*A*t any given point in time, a manager usually has at least 3 issues on her table. Most of the time even more.

Probably the issues are of different types - one of them is related to organization structure, one is related to a customer request, and the third maybe about the new engineer we are thinking of hiring.

The PUPPET principles describe 90% of the management world.

You need to read it, understand it, train on it, and adopt it to your style and beliefs. If you do that well, you will be better than 90% of the managers out there.

There are books that claim they have it all. The entire tutorial, from 0 to 100 in 10 chapters.

I don't claim it. I think that this book gives you the most important tools, it provides clarity on the stuff that really matters.

The other 10% that are not covered here are a combination of multiple small things. Mastering these is the differentiation between a great manager and an exceptional one.

An exceptional manager needs to have the ability to always prioritize the work, the skill to do effective context switching, to master time management techniques; they need to have charisma; they are superb communicators, and they have presentation abilities; they know how to manage organization diplomacy, and they have the knowledge on how to build a team, how to resolve conflicts; they have the theoretical knowledge on agile methodologies, how should seasoned leaders overcome the "curse of knowledge" syndrome, and more and more.

However, the number of pages in this book is getting bigger, so my promise to you as to try and cover some of the 10% topics above in my future books.

FINAL PERSONAL NOTE FROM ME TO YOU:

This was my first book. It took me years to write it. It was so fun! I hope you've liked it. If you did, I'd really appreciate if you can take a few moments to write a review of it. Thank you!

Acknowledgements and disclaimer

First and foremost, I'd like to thank Limor the love of my life that without brainstorming with her, proof-editing, suggestions and support this book would never see daylight.

I would also like to thank Lital Hassine, Moran Shimron, Uri Nativ and Tali Messing who were beta readers and provided for insightful changes that made this book a bit more GA worthy.

Thank you, Udi Ledergor, for helping me to understand the world of publishing via Amazon Kindle.

Thank you, Annie Duke, for allowing me to share ideas from the amazing book "Thinking in Bets".

Thank you, Lara Hogan, Julia Grace and Monique Valcour that gave me permission, to use their tweets/posts/articles.

Lastly for all the folks I've met along the way and inspired me to write this. Thank you!

A short disclaimer, though all the stories in this book are based on true events, some of them were changed or mixed a tiny bit in order to crisp a point or to make it a more interesting test case.